VIDEOTEX JOURNALISM
Teletext, Viewdata, and the News

VIDEOTEX JOURNALISM
Teletext, Viewdata, and the News

David H. Weaver
Indiana University

LEA LAWRENCE ERLBAUM ASSOCIATES, PUBLISHERS
1983   Hillsdale, New Jersey   London

Lawrence Erlbaum Associates, Inc. Publishers
365 Broadway
Hillsdale, New Jersey 07642

Library of Congress Cataloging in Publication Data

Weaver, David H. (David Hugh), 1946–
  Videotex journalism.

  Bibliography: p.
  Includes index.
  1. Journalism—Data processing. 2. Videotex (Data
transmission system) 3. Teletext (Data transmission system). I. Title.
PN4784.E5W4   1983   070'.028'5   82-21094
ISBN 0-89859-263-1

Printed in the United States of America
10 9 8 7 6 5 4 3 2 1

To Gail, Quinn, and Lesley
—Who put up with the most.

Contents

Preface

The idea for this study of the impact of videotex technology on journalists and the news came from readings and discussions with several colleagues at Indiana University's School of Journalism during the spring and summer of 1979, as well as from my own interest in the broader effects of technology on journalism, originally spurred by Donald Shaw at the University of North Carolina ten years ago. Prompted by the interest of certain of my Indiana associates in the coming teletext and viewdata systems (most notably John Ahlhauser, George Alexander, and Timothy Stehle) and the concern by others about the effects of changing technology on journalism (Walter Jaehnig, Cleve Wilhoit, and Richard Gray in particular), I began to consider ways to study the likely effects of the newly emerging videotex technology on journalism.

Although nearly all previous studies of the effects of technology on both journalism and the larger society were done long after the introduction of the technology (understandably!) and after its uses had become firmly established, it seemed worthwhile to try to assess some of the most likely major effects of an emerging technology *not* yet widely diffused, in the hope (perhaps naive) that the results of such a study might influence the ways in which this technology eventually would be employed.

While research on technological and marketing aspects of electronic delivery systems is necessary if such systems are to be developed and widely used, it is also extremely important to ask what effects such systems are having, or are likely to have, on the way journalists perform their jobs and on what comes to be defined as news. As H. M. Greenspun, publisher of the *Las Vegas Sun,* put it:

> With all the newfangled gadgetry we use today, there seems no end to the speed and
> efficiency with which we can package and distribute the news—the message. The state
> of the medium is on the cutting edge of technology; it's the message that's in jeop-
> ardy.[1]

England was the logical site for a study of the effects of videotex on journalism and the news because the Ceefax (BBC) and Oracle (ITV) teletext
systems have been operating as full-fledged public news and information
services longer than anywhere else in the English-speaking world (since 1974
for Ceefax and 1975 for Oracle). In addition, another system operated by
the Post Office (British Telecomm) since 1979 links individual television sets
to a computerized information bank via telephone lines and thus enables the
viewer to interact with the system. This viewdata system, known as Prestel,
offers more than 180,000 "pages" (TV screens or frames) of information
from more than 500 information providers (mostly businesses of various
kinds). More discussion on these systems follows in Chapter 1.

By comparison, the United States and other countries have been well
behind the United Kingdom in the development and use of both teletext and
viewdata. In addition to Britain's advantage over other countries in experience with real public videotex systems, the country is an especially
suitable research setting for studies of national media organizations and
journalists because of its centralized media patterns and relatively small
geographic area. All of the public teletext and viewdata systems in the country are based in London, as well as the television networks and national
newspapers.

Another great advantage of having England as a base for a study such as
this is the presence of such mass communication scholars as Jay Blumler,
director of the Centre for Television Research at the University of Leeds;
Peggy Gray, Philip Elliott, and James Halloran of the Centre for Mass
Communication Research at the University of Leicester; Jeremy Tunstall of
The City University in London; and Michael Gurevitch of The Open
University, to name just a few. Jay Blumler generously provided office
space in his Centre and helped arrange housing in Leeds during my stay
there from January until May of 1981. He introduced me to executives
working for the British Broadcasting Corporation, the Independent Television Network, and the Post Office's Prestel viewdata system. His sound advice on a wide ranging array of matters was absolutely essential to the com-
pletion of this study, and his reactions to some of the early drafts greatly
improved this report. In addition, his friendship made the transition from
the New World to the Old much easier and more pleasant.

In Leicester, Peggy Gray and James Halloran generously provided a copy

---

[1]H.M. Greenspun, "Guarding Our Most Precious Freedom," American Newspaper
Publishers Association, *Research Institute Bulletin, No. 1324* (August 13, 1979), p. 225.

of their extensive study of Prestel users in Swindon and Norwich, and Philip Elliott spent considerable time going over computer printouts from his national survey of nearly 400 journalists. Peter Golding kindly invited me to conduct a seminar on what I had found up to the time of leaving England, and several persons attending made helpful suggestions.

In the Netherlands, Harold de Bock, director of audience research at the Netherlands Broadcasting Foundation, spent many hours translating results from surveys of Dutch teletext users for me, and introduced me to the director of teletext services, W. P. G. Stokla. Dr. de Bock also helped me better my understanding of the Dutch culture and media system, for which I am deeply grateful. Through his efforts I was able to expand the study from the UK to the Netherlands and to Belgium.

In the Federal Republic of Germany, Werner and Blanca Degenhardt of the Institute for Communications Research at the University of Munich were especially helpful in arranging an interview with the manager of the Work Group for Communications Study, Frank Schumacher, and in translating key sections of a German study on the structure, scope, and commercial potential of viewdata.

Back in the United States, Indiana University provided the sabbatical leave that enabled me to spend nearly five months in England and Europe. Richard Gray, dean of the School of Journalism, fully supported this leave by arranging for my teaching and administrative duties to be handled by others in the School. Cleve Wilhoit, with the help of Inez Woodley and Jeff Black, kept the Bureau of Media Research going in fine form during my absence. And the John and Mary Markle Foundation provided a generous grant to cover my research and travel expenses, thanks to the interests of its president, Lloyd Morrisett and program officer Mary Milton.

To all of these persons, and many more who spent their valuable time answering my innumerable questions, I owe a great debt of gratitude. Without their help, and without the support of my university and family, this study could not have been completed. It must be remembered, however, that the conclusions drawn here are mine, and that others are not responsible for any errors of fact or judgment contained in this report.

David H. Weaver
School of Journalism
Indiana University

1 Videotex, Teletext, and Viewdata: A Brief Introduction

Much has been written and spoken in the past few years about delivering printed information electronically to television screens.[1] Nearly everyone agrees that such delivery will become more widespread than it is now, but there is much less agreement on what kinds of information will be available, how it will be paid for, how it will be delivered (over-the-air, by telephone line, by cable, or by fiber optics), and what effects it will have on existing media, especially such printed media as newspapers and magazines. There is

---

[1]See, for example, John W. Ahlhauser, "The Electronic Newspaper: U.S. Editors' Reactions to Teletext," *Center for New Communications Research Report* No. 9 (Bloomington, Indiana: School of Journalism, 1979); Tony Rimmer, "VIEWDATA—Interactive Television, with Particular Emphasis on the British Post Office's PRESTEL," paper presented to the 1979 annual meeting of the Association for Education in Journalism, Houston, Texas; "Teletext: TV Gets Married to the Printed Word," *Broadcasting,* August 20, 1979, pp. 30–36; "TV Systems Enabling Viewers to Call Up Printed Data Catch Eye of Media Firms," *The Wall Street Journal,* July 24, 1979, p. 40; "TV Turns to Print," *Newsweek,* July 30, 1979, pp. 73–75; "Videotex: Words on the TV Screen," *InterMedia,* 7: 6–53 (May 1979); Rex Winsbury, *The Electronic Bookstall: Push–button Publishing on Videotex* (London: International Institute of Communications, 1979); Anthony Smith, *Goodbye Gutenberg: The Newspaper Revolution of the 1980's* (New York, Oxford: Oxford University Press, 1980); *Prestel 1980* (London: Post Office Telecommunications, 1980); *Inside Videotex: Proceedings of a Seminar Held March 13–14, 1980* (Toronto, Canada: Infomart, 1980); "Electronic Publishing: The Newspaper of the Future?" Report by the Associated Press Managing Editors Media Competition Committee, November 1980; *VIDEOTEX '81: International Conference & Exhibition* (Middlesex, United Kingdom: Online Conferences, 1981); and John W. Ahlhauser, ed., *Electronic Home News Delivery: Journalistic and Public Policy Implications* (Bloomington, Indiana: School of Journalism and Center for New Communications, 1981).

also very little known about how such videotex systems are affecting, or might affect, journalistic values and work.

This present study attempts to provide some fairly specific answers to the questions of the impact of videotex systems on journalists and their work, on the flow of news and information in a society, and on other media and their policies. These answers are based on observations of and interviews with journalists working for the longest-lived public teletext systems in the world (the British Broadcasting Corporation's Ceefax system and the Independent Televisions's Oracle system), the British Post Office's Prestel viewdata system, and the Netherlands Broadcasting Foundation's "teletekst" system. In addition, interviews were conducted with key executives of these systems and with several communication researchers studying viewdata and teletext systems in the Federal Republic of Germany. Finally, the news content of the Ceefax and Oracle system was compared to the content of the BBC television nightly news and various newspapers in England, and numerous studies of teletext and viewdata systems were reviewed.

This book questions the claim that teletext and viewdata are dramatically new media, and it examines a number of technological, political, and economic factors that interfere with videotex's present contribution to high quality journalism and to the functioning of democratic forms of government. But the results of this study also suggest that videotex systems may become news media that are readily available and widely relied upon for the latest in local, national, and international news.

It seems clear that for videotex systems to realize their full potential as journalistic media, more attention must be paid to reporting news as well as to delivering it, to providing meaningful career opportunities for journalists, to finding ways to increase the length of news reports without straining the eyes and the patience of readers, to alerting readers to the full range of news content quickly, to allowing easy browsing through the "pages" of these systems, to keeping the costs low enough that nearly all can afford their daily diet of news, and to insuring that a wide variety of information and news is provided.

These recommendations assume that teletext and viewdata will become mass media, as television and newspapers are today, but at this point there is no assurance of such widespread adoption. The television still appears to be viewed by most as an entertainment medium, and newspaper information is still less expensive than the same information delivered to the TV screen by a viewdata system. On the other hand, the costs of newspapers and other printed media continue to climb sharply, whereas the costs of electronic delivery show signs of decreasing dramatically. At some point in the not too distant future, economics may favor electronic delivery of many kinds of information, including news.

But if electronically delivered news is to be as readily available, comprehensive, original, and convenient as is news currently printed in high quality newspapers and news magazines, major changes will have to be made in reporting practices, screen formats, organization of content, number of pages, costs, and economic bases of existing teletext and viewdata systems.

At present, the British teletext and viewdata systems—the oldest public systems in the world—are not dramatically new media. They do not provide much, if any, information or news not available from existing media; the choice and volume of news are very limited; journalists working for these systems do almost no original reporting; the news carried on the systems tends to be very superficial and event-oriented; the systems themselves are not strikingly new in their appeal to different senses; they have not had much impact on other media; they are more difficult and expensive to use for casual reading than printed media; and they (especially the more expensive viewdata receivers) are not diffusing among the public nearly as quickly as predicted.

In spite of these limitations, teletext and viewdata have provided more speed, convenience (for short news items and some statistics), and viewer choice for their relatively few users than have some existing media, if not better news coverage. In addition, audience surveys in Britain and the Netherlands indicate that those who have teletext and viewdata TV sets refer to them often for news and are generally satisfied with what they get.

Although this study cannot provide a crystal ball through which to see the future of videotex, it does provide a picture of the journalistic aspects, the kind of news, and the audience reactions to existing systems in Britain and the Netherlands. In doing so, it follows the lead of others who have looked at the way various developments in technology have influenced journalism and the news of the day.

A BRIEF HISTORICAL BACKGROUND

Past developments in technology have had significant, often unexpected, effects on the role of the journalist in society and the kind of information considered newsworthy. Nineteenth-century technological developments helped to turn the press into a mass audience medium and contributed to the broadening of the concept of "news" from the mercantile and the political to the experiences of more "common" people, especially those recorded in reports from the police and the courts. The telegraph, which newspapers began using in the 1840s to bring in timely outside news, had a significant impact on news values. A study of the Wisconsin English daily press from 1852 to 1916 by Donald Shaw suggests that political news "bias" (defined in terms of the number of value–laden words present in the news story) dropped dramatically in the 1880–1884 period during which there was a large increase in the proportion of wire service news used.[2] Shaw's analysis of the news coming in by telegraph showed that it contained significantly fewer value–laden words than the news provided by the newspapers' own reporters or that clipped from other papers or other sources.

Telegraph news also appeared to influence journalistic writing techniques and the scope of news coverage. Reporters learned to imitate the more "objective" news style of the wire services and to write news stories in the "inverted pyramid" style, with the "who, what, where, when, why, and how" crammed into the first few paragraphs for quicker and less costly telegraph transmission. Telegraph news also appeared to alter audience members' pictures of the political world in Shaw's study because the news stories after 1884 much more often pertained to a political candidate himself, regardless of where he was located, than about the supporters of the candidate located in Wisconsin or surrounding states.[3] In other words, the readers were taken more directly to the political event, regardless of whether or not it occurred in their part of the country. Thus, the telegraph enlarged the daily newspaper's area of coverage to the nation and the world, and seemed to heighten the public's desire for more timely national and international news.

Other technologies have had major effects on journalism and journalists, as well as on the larger society. In 1877, the telephone was used to send newspaper dispatches. It soon became a way not only of transmitting news, along with the telegraph, but also a way of collecting news from various faceless news sources both near and far who could more easily avoid reporters than in face-to-face encounters. With the increase in news gathering and transmitting capabilities came the invention of a device in the mid-1880s to simplify and speed up the mechanical processing of news—the Linotype machine. Twenty years later, the development of the vacuum tube opened the way for voice broadcasting, and the first American radio stations began to seek regular public listenership in the 1920s, with the result that the journalist's voice became nearly as important, perhaps more so, as his ability to gather information accurately and quickly.

In 1927, Bell Telephone Laboratories publicly demonstrated black and white television. After World War II, television took its place in most American and British homes, and it created a new kind of journalism where

---

[2]Donald L. Shaw, "News Bias and the Telegraph: A Study of Historical Change," *Journalism Quarterly,* 44 (Spring 1967), pp. 3-12, 31; and Donald L. Shaw, "Technology: Freedom for What?" in Ronald T. Farrar and John D. Stevens, eds., *Mass Media and the National Experience* (New York: Harper & Row, 1971), pp. 73-79.

[3]*Ibid.*

not only the voice, but also the looks, of the journalists are important, and where the visual aspects of an event or issue play a large part in the determination of its newsworthiness.

In short, it is clear that the technological developments of the nineteenth and twentieth centuries have contributed greatly to the creation of printed and electronic media capable of very quick dissemination of information to enormous audiences. But in providing the means to distribute more messages to more people faster, these technological developments have also changed the nature of these messages and the role of journalists in society. If teletext and viewdata systems come into widespread use, it is likely that they, too, will change the nature of news and journalism. This study attempts to shed some light on what kinds of changes are most likely.

VIDEOTEX

Before reviewing what some of the other studies of electronic delivery of information have found, it's necessary to clarify a few terms used throughout this report and much of the English-speaking world. As Rex Winsbury[4] points out, there is no internationally accepted terminology for this relatively new technology, but the International Telecommunication Union has agreed that the word *videotex* should be used for electronic systems that use a modified television set to display computer-based information.

TELETEXT

Those videotex systems that rely on a broadcast signal to reach television sets are known in the United Kingdom and many other countries as *teletext* (or "broadcast videotex") systems. The British Broadcasting Corporation's *Ceefax* ("see-facts") system and the *Oracle* ("optional reception of announcements by coded line electronics") system run by the independent television companies in the United Kingdom are both teletext systems. They are not interactive because the viewer cannot send messages directly back to the computer that stores and disseminates the information, but they do enable the viewer to choose certain "pages" (or screensful) of information for display on his or her television screen for as long as needed. These pages of information are constantly cycling in the air on top of the regular TV broadcast signal, and by pushing a certain page number on a keypad that looks like a small calculator the viewer can cause a specially equipped televi-

---

[4]Rex Winsbury, *The Electronic Bookstall: Push-button Publishing on Videotex* (London: International Institute of Communications, 1979), p. 3.

sion set to "grab" a particular page from the cycle and hold it for as long as needed.

Presently, teletext systems such as Ceefax and Oracle tend to be limited to 200 to 300 pages per TV channel because they rely on only two lines in the vertical blanking interval of the 625-line television signal in the United Kingdom (525 lines in the United States). These two lines are not used to transmit the regular TV image, so viewers don't notice any difference in their TV pictures until they switch to "Text" on their keypads. Using only two lines means that only about four pages per second can be transmitted; thus an entire cycle of 200 pages takes about 50 seconds or close to one minute to transmit. In practice, though, key pages such as the news, sports, and finance headlines are inserted in the sequence several times and therefore appear very quickly after being called. Because the pages tend to be grouped into "magazines" on both the BBC and Independent Television systems, and because these magazines generally consist of 100 or fewer pages, the actual wait for a news page is never longer than 25 seconds on Ceefax and only slightly more than that on Oracle. The BBC has recently begun using two extra lines for Ceefax, or a total of four, which halves the waiting time for pages.

The number of pages available on a teletext system such as Ceefax or Oracle could be greatly expanded if an entire TV channel were devoted to the system, rather than just two lines. If an entire channel were used, about 600 pages a second could be transmitted, or 18,000 in a half minute.[5] But, of course, there would be no regular television available on that channel. Such a system could be used after normal TV broadcasting hours to transmit large amounts of specialized information which could be stored by a special TV set with a memory device or, in the case of a cable television system where channels are plentiful, an entire channel could be devoted to a teletext system.

At present, the two aforementioned public teletext systems in the United Kingdom reach more than 300,000 specially equipped television receivers, making them the largest and the oldest (since 1974) public teletext systems in the world. In addition to news headlines and 20 or so brief news stories, there is also information about sports, finance, weather, travel, some food prices, recipes, and television and radio programs, films, records, and books. And Ceefax on BBC's Channel 2 also offers longer news background stories (usually four to six pages in length). (See Appendix 1 for a listing of Ceefax and Oracle contents.)

As of January 1981, a teletext TV set in the United Kingdom cost about £100 (200 to 250 dollars, depending on exchange rates) more to buy than a

---

[5]Walter Ciciora, "Teletext Systems: Considering the Prospective User," *Society of Motion Picture and Television Engineers (SMPTE) Journal,* 89: 846–849 (November 1980), p. 846.

comparable ordinary TV, or an extra £3–£4 a month to rent.[6] Adaptors to convert some ordinary TV sets to teletext sets are also available in the UK at various prices, and it is estimated that the price of both sets and adaptors will fall with increased production. Once a viewer has a TV set equipped to receive teletext, there is no additional charge for using teletext as often as one wants.

VIEWDATA

Those videotex systems that rely on a telephone line or cable (or, perhaps in the future, optical fibers) to reach television sets are known in the United Kingdom and many other countries as *viewdata* (or "interactive videotex") systems. The British Post Office (actually British Telecom) operates an interactive telephone-based viewdata system known as *Prestel* ("press-tell") that reaches about 13,000 specially equipped television sets, nearly 90% owned by businesss, with about 200,000 pages of information.[7] The Prestel system, operating since March 1979, is billed as "the world's first viewdata service"[8] by the British Post office and was accessible to most telephone owners via a local call to one of 19 different computers located throughout the United Kingdom (the number of computers has since been cut to two or three). Unlike the teletext systems of Ceefax and Oracle, the Prestel viewdata system does permit the viewer to respond directly to one of the computers that stores and disseminates the information. Thus a viewdata system such as Prestel can be used for recording viewers' frequency of use of certain pages of information, answers to certain questions, orders for certain goods and services advertised on the system, reservations for hotel rooms or airline seats, etc. Although the interactive capability of the Prestel viewdata system is not highly developed at this time,[9] the potential is there for such services as electronic banking, utility meter readings, electronic mail delivery, electronic voting, remote calculating and computer timesharing, etc.

Even though the interactive capability of Prestel is not highly developed now, the system provides much more information (more than 180,000 pages) than teletext systems such as Ceefax and Oracle. Much of this additional information is, however, business and commercial in nature, ranging

---

[6] *Which?* (January 1981), p. 8.

[7] Prestel "Superstats" for the month ending February 28, 1981.

[8] *Prestel 1980* (London: Post Office Telecommunications, 1980), p. 6.

[9] Tony Rimmer, "VIEWDATA—Interactive Television, with Particular Emphasis on the British Post Office's PRESTEL," paper presented to the 1979 annual meeting of the Association for Education in Journalism, Houston, Texas, pp. 3–5. See also Hilary Thomas, "VIDEOTEX: Review of the Year," *InterMedia*, 7: 27–29 (November 1979), p. 29.

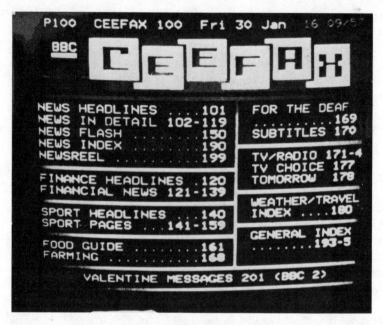

(Above) Index to the BBC's Ceefax Teletext System.

(Below) Index to the Independent Television Network's Oracle Teletext System.

(Above) Index to the Netherlands Broadcasting Foundation's Teletext System.

from accounting standards to labor statistics to shipping services to zinc statistics.[10] But there is still a considerable amount of information of more general interest, including pages on amusements, antiques, baby care, camping, dining out, employment and jobs, ferries, games, hobbies, news, painting, recreation, swimming, theatres, weather, and wine, to name just a few.[11] (See Appendix 2 for a listing of Prestel contents.) This information is not provided by the British Post Office, but rather by about 500 information providers (IPs) who lease pages from the Post Office. These IPs are mainly commercial organizations such as Abbey Life Group (insurance), Barclay's Bank, Holiday Inn Hotels, Pan American World Airways, Volkswagen, etc., with a few non-commercial organizations such as the Arts Council of Great Britain, the British Broadcasting Corporation, the Birmingham Public Libraries, the British Red Cross, Middlesex Polytechnic, and the Universities Central Council on Admissions.[12] In reality, there are only about 140 "true" information providers to Prestel who lease pages in minimum quantities of 100 frames and who pay a £4000 service charge per year and £4 per frame per year rental.

In addition, these IPs rent editing terminals from the Post Office at about £2000 a year and employ staff persons to design and update pages on

[10]*Prestel Business Directory* (October 1980), pp. 1–24.

[11]*The Prestel User,* 4: 1–116 (January 1981), pp. 7–44.

[12]*Ibid.,* pp. 49–73.

Prestel.[13] The other 360 or so organizations that provide information to Prestel are known as "sub-IPs" because they pay some of the IPs (known as "umbrella IPs") to create and update smaller blocks of pages for them, and thus avoid some of the costs associated with renting larger blocks of pages, editing terminals, and paying keyboard operators.

Just as it is not terribly cheap to become an information provider to the Prestel viewdata system, it is also not cheap to use Prestel, as compared to using Ceefax and Oracle. Most television sets equipped to receive Prestel cost £450–£500 more than a regular color TV, or just about double what a regular set costs, whereas most teletext sets cost about £100 above the normal price.[14] Prestel sets usually cost about £15 a month more to rent than do regular TV sets (£10–£12 a month), whereas teletext sets cost an extra £3–£4 more. Unlike teletext, the use of Prestel also involves charges for the use of the Prestel computer (about 3 pence per minute during the business day), the use of the telephone at normal rates (which include charges for local calls as well as long-distance ones), and the use of certain pages on Prestel that may cost up to 50 pence apiece, depending on the whims of the information provider.[15]

Probably in large part because of the rather high costs of providing information to Prestel and using the system, it has become mostly a business information service in the two years of its public operation and the marketing strategy, under the new director Richard Hooper, has shifted away from concentrating on the home user to concentrating on business users.[16] As of February 1981, nearly one-half of the 7971 users were located in the London area and nearly 88% of them were classified as "business" rather than "residential."[17] But Hooper argues that the British Post Office has not forgotten about the domestic, or home, market for Prestel—just postponed the push for this market until the last half of the 1980s.[18]

---

[13]*Prestel Handbook* II, 2: 1–191 (June 1980), pp. 101–102.

[14]*Which?* (January 1981), p. 8.

[15]*Prestel Handbook* II, pp. 153–154.

[16]Personal interview with Richard Hooper, director of Prestel, in London, March 16, 1981. See also Peter Stothard, "Why instant information is slow to catch on," *The Sunday Times,* 25 January 1981, p. 61; and Judy Redfearn, "Viewdata Systems: Battle Joined," *Nature,* 291: 182 (21 May 1981).

[17]Prestel "Superstats," February 6, 1981.

[18]Personal interview with Richard Hooper, director of Prestel, in London, March 16, 1981. This point was also made in a personal interview with Peter Wynne-Davies, Publicity, Prestel, in London, February 6, 1981. Hooper argued in an article in the May 1979 issue of *InterMedia,* pp. 17–21, that "Prestel can only be comprehended as a mass medium. By a mass medium, one means that significant numbers of people will access a small number of pages frequently, as distinct from small numbers of people accessing large numbers of pages infrequently. From the very beginning, in the early 1970s, within the Post Office's research department, Prestel (or Viewdata as it was called then) was developed as a mass medium for the residential and business market." (p. 18)

OTHER SYSTEMS

Even though the British teletext systems, Ceefax and Oracle, and the British viewdata system, Prestel, are the oldest public videotex systems, they are certainly not the only systems being operated and tested in the world today. At least 12 other countries are testing and/or operating videotex systems, and the list keeps growing. These include Australia, Belgium, Canada, Finland, France, West Germany, Japan, the Netherlands, Sweden, Switzerland, Venezuela, and the United States. According to the introduction to the proceedings of Videotex '81, a major international conference held in Toronto, Canada, from May 20-22, 1981, "more than 1000 companies are active in the field" and "important developments in the technology take place almost every week."[19]

In a review in May 1979 of 22 national videotex systems from Australia, Canada, Finland, France, West Germany, Japan, Sweden, the United Kingdom, and the United States, the International Institute of Communications' magazine, *InterMedia,* classified one-half of these systems as "teletext" and the other half as "videotex" (or viewdata).[20] In almost every case, the teletext systems were being tested by broadcasters or broadcasting organizations, and the viewdata systems were being introduced by a government post office or ministry of telecommunications. Thus, the teletext systems were more likely to be backed by private (or, in a few cases, public) broadcasting organizations, and the viewdata systems were more likely to be backed by government agencies. This is not true in the U.S., however, where nearly all viewdata and teletext trials are being conduced by private firms.[21]

Another review in 1979 by Rex Winsbury of 25 systems being tested and/or operated in Australia, France, Germany, the Netherlands, Japan, Sweden, the United Kingdom, and the United States classified 13 of these systems as viewdata and 12 of them as teletext.[22] Of the 13 viewdata systems, six were based on British Prestel technology and located in the UK, West Germany, the Netherlands, and the United States. Four systems (all in France) were based on the French Antiope technology, and the remaining four systems were based on some other kind of technology.

In a more recent review of videotex standards in Western Europe presented to the Videotex '81 conference in Toronto in May 1981, G. H. L. Childs of the Viewdata Development Section of the British Telecommunica-

---

[19] *VIDEOTEX '81: International Conference & Exhibition* (Middlesex, United Kingdom: Online Conferences, 1981), p. v.

[20] *InterMedia,* 7 (May 1979), pp. 8-9.

[21] See *Editor & Publisher,* June 26, 1982, pp. 41-47, and *Broadcasting,* June 28, 1982, pp. 37-49, for a review of U.S. videotex ventures.

[22] Rex Winsbury, *The Electronic Bookstall: Push-button Publishing on Videotex,* p. 69-74.

tions Research Laboratories argued that the Prestel viewdata display standard was being used for a public or test service, or had been adopted for a proposed test service, in Austria, Denmark, Finland, West Germany, Italy, the Netherlands, Norway, Spain, Sweden, Switzerland, and the United Kingdom, whereas the French Antiope display standard has been adopted only in France.[23] As for teletext, Childs argued that the British standard had been adopted in Austria, northern Belgium, Denmark, Finland, West Germany, the Netherlands, Sweden and the United Kingdom, whereas the French standard had been adopted in France. According to Childs, Italy intends to broadcast a teletext test service that alters between the British and French standards week by week.[24]

But even though the British have a commanding lead in Western Europe in getting their viewdata and teletext standards accepted by other countries, the French, Canadians, and the American Telephone & Telegraph Company (AT&T) announced at the Videotex '81 conference that they had agreed on a videotex standard that would be compatible with and supported by the French Antiope and the Canadian Telidon systems.[25] This agreement may mean that most of the United States systems (especially the viewdata) will employ either French or Canadian hardware, rather than British, even though some of the U.S. systems today rely on the hardware and software of the Prestel, Ceefax, and Oracle systems.

---

[23]G. H. L. Childs, "The Situation on Videotex Standards in Europe," *VIDEOTEX '81*, p. 385. See also Peter Large, "European standard on viewdata is emerging," *The Guardian*, March 17, 1981, p. 16.

[24]Childs, p. 386.

[25]Childs, p. 378, argues that "the only real area of incompatibility" between the proposed French Antiope test service and the British Prestel system "lies in the way in which attributes are applied to graphic characters." But whereas the diferences between Prestel and Antiope may not be too great, because the graphic displays of both are built on the screen from tiny squares (an alpha-mosaic system), the differences between these systems and the Canadian Telidon system are considerably greater because the Telidon system is "alpha-geometric," meaning that it can display true curves built from geometric elements such as an arc, polygon, etc. The Telidon system can also display high–definition pictures in an "alpha–photographic" system. See also Hilary Thomas, "VIDEOTEX: Review of the Year," *InterMedia*, 7: 27-29 (November 1979), p. 27, and Peter Large, "European standard on viewdata is emerging," *The Guardian*, March 17, 1981, p. 16, for fairly clear non–technical explanations of the differences in these systems.

VideoPrint, a twice monthly newsletter focusing on teletext and videotex systems, claims in its May 22, 1981, issue that "the new AT&T protocol does not provide compatibility with the British Prestel viewdata representation. The exclusion of Prestel—particularly when Telidon and Antiope are at least partially supported—is a considerable blow to the future prospects for export of the British system. Not only will other U.S. organizations involved with videotex tend to shy away from Prestel, but other countries (Sweden, West Germany, etc.) will think twice about further involvement with what could become an 'orphan' technology."

SUMMING UP

In brief, then, the term "videotex" refers to any system of electronically transferring printed or graphic information from a computer to a television screen, whether by broadcast signal, telephone line, cable, or fiber optics. In the United Kingdom, and in this report, the term "teletext" refers to broadcast videotex systems such as Ceefax and Oracle, and the term "viewdata" refers to other more interactive videotex systems that permit viewer feedback through a telephone line or cable such as the Prestel system does.

Because this present study is set mainly in the United Kingdom, and therefore is based mainly on the Ceefax, Oracle and Prestel systems, it runs the risk of not being fully applied to other videotex systems of the world, especially those based on the French and Canadian technologies. Nevertheless, it is hoped that the findings on journalists and their work, the flow of news and information, and the impact on other media will be of interest and value to all those involved in some way with videotex systems, regardless of the technologies used. And it is further hoped that these findings may cause some re-evaluations of the roles of teletext and viewdata systems as providers of news and information before these roles become set in the concrete of economic and organizational structures.

2 Teletext and Viewdata: A Closer Look

Although there is little argument that the technology exists now in many countries for the widespread development of both teletext and viewdata systems, there is much speculation about the possible benefits and drawbacks of such systems for journalists, the larger society, and other media. Most of the thinking and writing with regard to the effects of teletext and viewdata is speculation and conjecture—not surprising given the relative newness and limited diffusion of videotex—and most of it can be classified as either "optimistic" or "pessimistic," with a few views in the "mixed reactions" camp. This chapter reviews some of these views of videotex and pulls together the harder evidence from some of the few systematic studies that presently exist.

THE OPTIMISTIC VIEW

Many of those writing about the possibilities of electronic information delivery, via teletext or viewdata systems, are unabashedly optimistic. They stress the ability of the viewer to select only information that is of interest, increased access for more points of view because of the relatively low cost of becoming an information provider, increased diversity of information resulting from low costs and nearly unlimited storage capacities, and greater power for the individual because of increased control over information received, and the ability to provide nearly instantaneous feedback to the sources of various messages.[1]

Many of these arguments about the merits of teletext and viewdata are reminiscent of some of the arguments for the quick adoption of other media, such as motion pictures, radio, and television. Advocates of these media predicted such benefits as increased access to information about current events, strengthened democracy and diminished class distinctions because of the uniformity of information available to all citizens, increased national unity and decreased isolation of all persons, establishment of national forums for political discussion, increased worldwide understanding and international unity, better education, and a better-informed electorate.[2]

The arguments in support of teletext and viewdata systems emphasize diversity of information, rather than uniformity, and individual control and convenience, rather than national unity. There is also an emphasis on the greatly increased *volume* of information that may be accessed in the privacy of one's home. As two journalism instructors from Brigham Young University put it, "The newshole of an electronic newspaper is limited only by the storage capacity of the computer system."[3] This claim was echoed recently by a North Carolina newspaper editor who wrote that "because computer memory space is cheaper than newsprint, stories can run as long as anyone wants them to."[4] A promotion brochure for teletext and viewdata systems in the United Kingdom emphasized that "viewdata will offer limitless specialized information and other services as well as general information."[5]

In addition to the "vast quantities" argument, a closely related theme is that of "immediate access." This claim is especially popular among advocates of teletext (broadcast) systems. As one promotional brochure for British teletext put it, "Teletext turns your television set into a storehouse of up-to-the-minute information, and puts it all instantly at your disposal—literally at your fingertips."[6] In his book, *American Newspapers*

---

[1]For a concise summary of these arguments, I am indebted to Linda Zaradich, a master's student in journalism at Indiana University, and particularly to a paper by her entitled "Electronic Home News Delivery: A Systems Analysis," written for a seminar on mass media and society in April 1981.

[2]See Robert Davis, "Response to Innovation: A Study of Popular Argument About New Mass Media," unpublished dissertation, University Microfilms Inc., Ann Arbor, Michigan, 1976.

[3]Cecelia Fielding and William C. Porter, "Time to turn on the newspaper," *The Quill: Magazine for Journalists,* 69 (April 1981), p. 18.

[4]Mark Ethridge III, "Report from Coral Gables: We can relax. Or can we?" *Electronic Publishing: The Newspaper of the Future?* (Report by the Associated Press Managing Editors Media Competition Committee, November 1980), p. 12.

[5]"Teletext and Viewdata for the World" (Basingstoke, England: Bell Carter Elliot Richards Limited, 1979), p. 1.

[6]"A British TV first! Teletext" (London: Department of Industry, undated), p. 1.

in the 1980s, Ernest Hynds writes that electronic home communication systems will "offer immediate access to vast quantities of information and instant news on demand."[7] A brochure describing the Independent Broadcasting Authority's Oracle teletext system makes this same point even more emphatically:

> As a news medium, ORACLE is ideal. Even for headlines, a conventional newspaper has a copy deadline some hours before actual publication: television can accept copy changes a few minutes before transmission. But ORACLE can be on the air with the latest news only seconds after a story breaks. It is difficult to think of a much better news service than that, and its use in this way could make it the most significant development in communications since Caxton.[8]

Colin McIntyre, editor of the BBC's Ceefax system, sees teletext as, "The quickest public information service any broadcaster has ever had at his command."[9] To support this argument, McIntyre points to Ceefax's coverage of the 1980 Moscow Olympics, where sub-editor Audrey Adams typed sports results and news stories directly into the Ceefax computer 1550 miles away, and to the "real-time" subtitling of President Ronald Reagan's inaugural speech on January 20, 1981, with no advance script, that enabled the Palantype (mechanical shorthand machine) operator to take account of ad-libs and corrections.[10]

McIntyre also asserts that "subtitling was the original trigger for the development of teletext,"[11] and this observation leads naturally to another argument for teletext and viewdata: That those who are deaf or hard-of-hearing will finally be able to enjoy television, whereas those who can hear normally will not be distracted by subtitles at the bottom of the screen. As McIntyre puts it, "All teletext is of benefit to the deaf and hard-of-hearing,"[12] and "can truly be described as revolutionary."[13] McIntyre points out that reading Ceefax before viewing the main BBC television evening news means that those who can't hear well, "will know that the tanks they see in the streets are in Beirut and not in Belfast, or vice-versa; and that the actress appearing on the screen has just arrived in London for a

---

[7]Ernest C. Hynds, *American Newspapers in the 1980s* (New York: Hastings House, 1980), p. 281.

[8]"ORACLE: Broadcasting the Written Word" (Basingstoke, England: Kempsters, undated), p. 5.

[9]Colin McIntyre, "CEEFAX—an editorial update," *European Broadcasting Union Review,* 32 (March 1981), p. 45.

[10]See Colin McIntyre, "BBC Ceefax Girl the Fastest in Moscow," Ceefax Paper, September 1980; Colin McIntyre, "The Palantype Experiment," Ceefax Paper BB/1, February 1981, pp. 1–6; and Colin McIntyre, "CEEFAX—an editorial update," pp. 46–47.

[11]McIntyre, "CEEFAX—an editorial update," p. 46.

[12]Colin McIntyre, "Making news more than just a picture for the deaf," *Viewdata Magazine,* 4 (July 1979), p. 10.

[13]Colin McIntyre, "Ceefax and the Hard of Hearing," Ceefax Briefing, undated.

film premiere, and has not died, or been divorced, or hijacked."[14] With teletext, McIntyre claims, "Deaf viewers are able to see their own written version of the news and read at their own individual speed, so that news subtitles become much less necessary."[15]

Still another argument in favor of teletext and viewdata is that these systems permit audience feedback and immediate action to be taken as a result. As McIntyre puts it, "The teletext audience is one of the most involved, most committed, most participating of audiences that I have met in 30 years."[16] Even with a one-way teletext system such as Ceefax, McIntyre writes that viewers "demand their say, all the time,"[17] and "we can correct the mistake, if mistake it was, before that very viewer's eyes, while he watches, accompanied for the purpose by admiring members of his family witnessing Daddy's correction of the foolish broadcaster."[18]

This capacity for audience feedback is, of course, considerably enhanced with interactive viewdata systems such as the British Post Office's Prestel. According to one *Sunday Times* writer:

> To the newcomer, Prestel is a marvel. Touch the pocket-calculator-like keyboard of your £600 Prestel set, and the Nine O'Clock News can become a bedtime story, an instant booking form for the Royal Shakespeare Theatre, or a six-color graph of the growth in sterling M3. You can buy with it, sell with it, and even use it to complain about it.[19]

Other possible uses of viewdata systems like Prestel include monitoring homes for fire and theft, providing an electronic school, electronic mail, library services from the home, and electronic funds transfer (banking), according to the Manitoba Telephone System which offers a videotex service to about 50 homes in South Headingley, Manitoba.[20] Still other uses of videotex are foreseen by the Viditel Project Manager of the Netherlands Postal and Telecommunications Services, including the conducting of public opinion polls and electronic voting and referendums.[21]

One of the most basic arguments of all, very possibly the most compelling for teletext and especially for viewdata systems, is economic. As Joseph

---

[14]McIntyre, "Making news more than just a picture," p. 10.

[15]McIntyre, "CEEFAX—an editorial update," p. 47.

[16]*Ibid.*, p. 44.

[17]*Ibid.*, p. 44.

[18]*Ibid.*, p. 45.

[19]Peter Stothard, "Why instant information is slow to catch on," *The Sunday Times*, 25 January 1981, p. 61.

[20]Brad Schultz, "Manitoba Town to Test Viewdata-Type Service," *Computerworld*, August 6, 1979, p. 34.

[21]P.J.G.M. Ruiten, "Videotex Developments in the Netherlands," *VIDEOTEX '81: International Conference & Exhibition* (Middlesex, United Kingdom: Online Conferences, 1981), p. 177.

Roizen, president of a consulting firm involved with both technologies, puts it, "We are looking at a multibillion-dollar industry that, over the next five years, will supplant our current means of telecommunications."[22] Roizen's view is echoed by Kenneth Baker, British Minister for Information Technology, who claims that information technology is going to be "the key growth sector in the British economy."[23]

In addition to the opportunities for *making* money, some of those getting involved with videotex, especially newspaper and magazine publishers, are doing so out of a fear of *losing* money. As one videotex project manager puts it, "There are always a number of information providers who participate simply because their competitors are taking part. Others take part because they are afraid of missing the boat once Viditel (the Dutch viewdata system) really gets going."[24] Donald Sparrow, director of a $600,000 study of electronic information systems by the consulting firm Arthur D. Little, Inc., reinforces this point when he asserts that newspapers are interested in electronic information systems for two reasons: "One is the potential threat to the newspapers, and the second is the potential opportunities to information providers."[25]

Another variant of the economic argument for videotex focuses on the *consumer* rather than the producer of information or the system operator. Martin Goldfarb, head of one of Canada's largest research firms, states that, "As costs go up, as they seem to, the availability of a piece of technology that actually lowers costs will attract consumers, not just to get involved, but to pushing the technocrats to getting on with making it better and more cost practical."[26] To Goldfarb, the cost of videotex is, or will be, "infinitesimally small when you place it in the context of the current cost of distribution of information, goods, and services."[27] George Cox, managing director of the London-based Butler, Cox, & Partners consulting firm, claims that the appeal of viewdata is "very nearly irresistible and it offers a real possibility for adding value to a user's TV."[28]

Another version of the economic argument contrasts the costs of printing information with distributing it electronically, and asserts that both the

[22]Harry F. Waters, Cynthia H. Wilson, and Peter Davies, "TV Turns to Print," *Newsweek,* July 30, 1979, p. 74.

[23]Chris Griffin-Beale, "UK pulls together to push teletext in U.S.," *Broadcast,* 2 March 1981, p. 17.

[24]P.J.G.M. Ruiten, "Videotex Developments in the Netherlands," p. 176.

[25]Bill Kelly, "All The News That's Fit to Compute," *Washington Journalism Review,* April 1980, p. 16.

[26]Martin Goldfarb, "Videotex 2000: Prophesy and Prognosis," *Inside Videotex: Proceedings of a Seminar Held March 13–14, 1980* (Toronto, Canada: Infomart, 1980), p. 118.

[27]*Ibid.,* p. 118.

[28]Don Leavitt, "Study Pinpoints Six Issues Raised by Viewdata," *Computerworld,* February 19, 1979, p. 10.

publishers and the consumers will benefit from eliminating the printing process. Bill Kelly, a Washington free-lance writer, predicts that the electronic newspaper will, "not only be affordable to the reader, but will eventually be cheaper to produce for the publisher."[29] Kelly argues, as do others, that the environmental effects and huge energy requirements of producing and printing newsprint are increasing its costs and diminishing its availability, thus making the elimination of the printing process "a logical step in the history of the industry."[30] He asserts that a single Sunday edition of the New York Times consumes 62,860 trees at the same time that electronic component costs and magnetic storage costs are dropping dramatically. This makes the economics of the electronic newspaper look better "almost by the day."[31] Richard Hooper, director of Prestel, agrees and talks of the "cross-over point" at which the costs of print exceed the costs of distributing information electronically because of the rising costs of materials, energy, and the dipping costs of electrons.[32]

These, then, are the main arguments in favor of teletext and viewdata: Vast quantities of very diverse information will be available cheaply and immediately to nearly all persons (even those deaf or hard-of-hearing) who can respond almost instantly in a variety of ways (including buying and selling goods and services, making reservations, sending messages, transferring money, etc.) using electronic systems that will become huge and profitable industries in themselves. Teletext and viewdata will save energy and result in less damaging effects on the environment than the printing process. As one British publisher recently put it, commenting on the excitement surrounding the development of Prestel in 1977:

> In those dewy-eyed days viewdata promised to be all things to all people; it would revolutionise everybody's life at home, at work and at study. It would allow all points of view to be brought to all, open up society, and do virtually everything except find a cure for cancer. "Better information" was the cry; "accessibility by all" was the message; and for an entry fee of some £2,000 anybody could launch the equivalent of a national newspaper.[33]

Even though there may be "every reason for optimism," in the words of one videotex project manager,[34] there are also many arguments for a more restrained, even pessimistic, view of teletext and viewdata.

---

[29]Kelly, "All The News That's Fit to Compute," p. 16.
[30]*Ibid.*, p. 16.
[31]*Ibid.*, p. 16.
[32]Personal interview with Richard Hooper, director of Prestel, in London, March 16, 1981.
[33]Peter Head, "Prestel—from the Point of View of One Information Provider," *VIDEOTEX '81: International Conference & Exhibition* (Middlesex, United Kingdom: Online Conferences, 1981), p. 138.
[34]P.J.G.M. Ruiten, "Videotex Developments in the Netherlands," p. 177.

THE PESSIMISTIC VIEW

Perhaps one of the most fundamental criticisms of teletext and viewdata is that they are examples of "technological push" rather than "market pull"—that is, there is "as yet very little real evidence that the consumer wants or needs this very different medium."[35] In other words, it may be that electrical engineers have invented something for which there is no real need that is not already well satisfied by more conventional forms of communication such as the printed page, the telephone, and the television. As one German spokesman put it:

> It remains to be seen whether and to what extent the public will use the new services. If the public does use them, everybody will take that for a proof that there is a real need for these services. There is room for suspicion, however, that in the field of electronic communication more often than not the service does not answer a need but the need is created by the service. The secret pacemaker of society's heartbeat is the technician.[36]

Even among information providers to the British Prestel system, there is debate about where viewdata systems fit into the existing information order and which needs they should be trying to meet. In reacting to the change in marketing strategy of Prestel from the general domestic to the more specific business, the "inview" newsletter of Mills & Allen Communications notes that "Prestel is a very general system not well suited to the particular. It is not for example, a real-time system but a system requiring update and inherently incapable of minute to minute accuracy."[37] And the newsletter concludes that "the Gateway—using Prestel as a way into private computer systems—is Prestel's only real hope of a long-term role in the specialist business viewdata market."[38]

An even more global argument against the widespread adoption of teletext, viewdata, and other new technologies is made by Philip Elliott of Leicester University:

> The thesis I wish to advance is that what we are seeing and what we face is a continuation of the shift away from involving people in society as political citizens of nation states towards involving them as consumption units in a corporate world.[39]

---

[35]Gerald Haslam, "Videotex: What is it and where does it fit?" *Inside Videotex: Proceedings of a Seminar Held March 13-14, 1980* (Toronto, Canada: Infomart, 1980), p. 10.

[36]Hans Kimmel, "Germany: A Battle Between Broadcasters and the Press," *InterMedia*, 7:39-40 (May 1979), p. 40.

[37]"One year on...," *Inview, 4* (April 1981), p. 1.

[38]*Ibid.*

[39]Philip Elliott, "Will There Be News in 1991?" Paper presented at a seminar on Manipulation in Mass Communication sponsored by the Foundation for Mass Communication Research, Koningshof Veldhoven, The Netherlands, March 25-27, 1981, pp. 2-3.

Elliott sees a "sleight of hand" in the arguments of Daniel Bell and others who look forward to an explosion of information and communication, and who claim that new technologies such as teletext and viewdata will increase general access to information and open up new possibilities of two-way communication. He argues that access to information is dependent upon the way this information is accumulated and catalogued, and that access from the home will encourage the "privatisation of information," resulting in groups of people who have no other connection with each other than their common use of the same information service. In this way people are more susceptible to manipulation, in Elliott's view, and are deprived of the possibility of answering back because they have fewer opportunities for association in which common needs might be recognized and demands formulated. This view, also known as the "enclave theory," envisions "a nation of new isolationists who are removed from all but the most basic human intercourse in their all-electronic caves."[40]

Elliott is also critical of the claim that people will have access to much more information with new technologies than they do now, because in his opinion, much of what is called "information" on these new systems does not supply the knowledge and opinion necessary to foster informed decision-making in a democracy. Rather, much of the content has a "high level of symbolic, mythical content and passive entertainment value."[41] In other words, much of the content of the British mass market daily newspapers (and presumably of teletext and viewdata systems as well) is "interesting" news, rather than "important" news that "exaggerates the commonalities between people and plays down structural divisions of interest," rather than being concerned with "institutions, organizations and decision-making in society."[42]

James Carey and John Quirk echo Elliott's concern in calling for a distinction between information and knowledge. They maintain that knowledge "can be manipulated like any other commodity" by not only controlling factual information or data, but also by controlling a system of thought, or paradigm, that determines what the standards are for assessing the truth and defining knowledge.[43] "Instead of creating a 'new future,' modern technology invites the public to participate in a ritual of control where fascination with technology masks the underlying factors of politics

---

[40]Harry F. Waters, Cynthia H. Wilson, and Peter Davies, "TV Turns to Print," *Newsweek,* July 30, 1979, p. 75.

[41]Elliott, *op. cit.,* p. 4.

[42]Elliott, *op. cit.,* p. 5.

[43]James W. Carey & John J. Quirk, "The History of the Future," in George Gerbner, Larry P. Gross, & William H. Melody, eds., *Communications Technology and Social Policy* (New York and London: John Wiley & Sons, 1973), p. 500.

and power," according to Carey and Quirk.[44] This is so, they assert, because to participate in computer-based information systems intelligently, "The citizen of the future will have to undergo a continuing, lifelong education in real time, the acquisition of new knowledge when it is needed in time to meet problems as they arise." And these "extraordinary demands" will merely "co-opt him into the technical apparatus with only the illusion of control."[45]

Closely related to this criticism is the charge that electronic information delivery systems, like many other forms of technology, will serve to support the existing political-economic power structures in various societies by co-opting people into believing they have a voice in the running of "the system" through the "two-way" capability of viewdata. By creating an "artificial demand" for teletext and viewdata services that will result in huge profits for media and electronics industries, by continuing to rely on relatively few "official" sources of news and information rather than presenting many views on many issues, and by providing more and more very brief news items that consist of what official sources have said or are doing about particular matters, the resulting "information overload" encourages greater specialization of interests and information-seeking patterns, which in turn contributes to the isolation of people from one another, and provides advertisers with more select audiences.[46]

This concern with increasing specialization is also reflected in the questions raised by those who believe in the value of incidental learning and "agenda-setting" from news media. As Charles Everill of Harte Hanks Communications succinctly puts it, electronic retrieval systems work most efficiently, "if the consumer knows exactly what (information) he wants, but so often we don't know what we want."[47] Jay Blumler elaborates on Everill's concern when he asks:

> But I wonder what will happen in the new communications era to those services, mainly provided today by the mass media and especially by the broadcast media, which cater for man in his most general role of all—for his role as a citizen of the nation state, who needs to be kept aware, not only of its main problems of the moment but also of issues preoccupying people beyond its borders in this increasingly interdependent world. Presumably we cannot automatically assume that the new communication technologies will serve that general citizen role well, first because its informational requirements are far more diffuse than those, say, of engineers, techni-

---

[44]*Ibid.*, p. 501.

[45]*Ibid.*, p. 499.

[46]Linda Zaradich, "Electronic Home News Delivery: A Systems Analysis," paper written for a seminar on mass media and society, School of Journalism, Indiana University, April 1981, pp. 3–13.

[47]Daniel Machalaba, "Hot off the Screen: More Publishers Beam Electronic Newspapers to Home Video Sets," *The Wall Street Journal*, January 2, 1981, p. 7.

cians, firemen trainees, shoppers, etc., and secondly, because it demands the existence of competent, responsible and well-resourced agents able to act for us by scanning the social and political environment and drawing our attention to what we need to know. Which button on the keyboard of his domestic computerized video-display screen should the citizen press in order to be kept in touch with the issues of the day?[48]

Blumler fears that electronic information delivery systems such as teletext and viewdata might lead to less public exposure to serious information on social and political questions, not only because of the ability of each person to select, but also because channel multiplication will probably mean a decreased share of the audience for any given news organization or channel, and this will mean, in turn, decreased revenue to support serious news-gathering efforts. He concludes that there is, therefore, a case for keeping developments in telecommunications technology under public policy review and regulation to guarantee strong, responsible, and free information agents to serve citizens well.[49]

The argument that teletext and viewdata systems are not well-suited for the presentation of serious social and political information is underscored by Prestel journalist Mike Bygrave, who asserts, "Prestel's encyclopedic nature is illusory. With all its hundreds of thousands of 'pages,' the system cannot actually cope with any lengthy or complex set of information."[50] Bygrave argues that Prestel (and presumably other viewdata systems) must be a highly selective information medium because of the limited capacity of each screenful (or page), and the cost of the people and hardware needed to input large volumes of information. Even with such people and hardware, Bygrave points out that the capacity of one page of Prestel (80 or 90 words) makes one ask "if it isn't going to distort (news) to the point of absurdity. Can you really present any serious issue fairly when you're working at that sort of length?"[51]

He is also skeptical about Prestel (or other viewdata systems) as journalistic media because, "It's hard to see how text on Prestel could be organized to pay. Most news or current affairs media pass on only a portion of their cost to the consumer, making the balance up in advertising revenue. Yet, it's not clear how a traditional 'package' of text and advertisements could work on Prestel."[52] Bygrave doubts further that anyone is even going to think seriously about advertising on viewdata systems until such systems have "succeeded" in terms of numbers of users. Thus, unless advertising does absorb a substantial portion of the costs associated with

---

[48]Jay G. Blumler, "Information Overload: Is There a Problem?" in Eberhard Witte, ed., *Human Aspects of Telecommunication* (New York: Springer-Verlag, 1980), pp. 233–34.

[49]*Ibid.*, pp. 234–35.

[50]Mike Bygrave, "Writing on an Empty Screen," *InterMedia,* 7: 26–28 (May 1979), p. 26.

[51]*Ibid.*, p. 27.

[52]*Ibid.*

teletext and viewdata systems (or unless there is significant support from government), Bygrave thinks that "there is so much free or dirt-cheap news and current affairs around already, who will pay to see more?"[53]

The concern with the ability of teletext and viewdata systems to present information of a lengthy or complex nature in a convenient manner is shared by others. It has been estimated that it would take approximately 70 videotex TV screenfuls to contain as many words as one page of a quality newspaper such as *The Wall Street Journal* does. Furthermore, one cannot take a television set as easily onto a subway or train, or carry it from place to place, as one can a newspaper. The limits of videotex systems in terms of number of words and portability are dramatically illustrated by Professor Edwin Diamond who challenges his engineering students at the Massachusetts Institute of Technology to:

> Design a communications system that is lightweight and easily portable, yet has a capacity of 60,000-100,000 words. Display screen should be no more than 9 inches and fit flat on a desk top. System should have easy access so that even an eight-year-old can plug it in. Should be storable and recallable in seconds. System should be usable in airplanes, autos, and canoes. Cost should be no more than $2 a unit.[54]

If the students succeed, Diamond notes, "Their invention would be the magazine."[55] Presumably, the same could be said for many quality newspapers. Their size would exceed the prescribed 9 inches, but their word capacity might be greater than 100,000 per issue.

There is also the question of the ease of reading from a television screen as compared to the ease of reading from the printed page. The letters on the screen are often not as sharply defined as those on the printed page, and there tends to be some movement or flickering of the letters on the TV screen. Although this question is still open, there are those such as deputy editor Tony Fowler of the *Daily Express* in London who argue, "Whatever happens in the realm of technology, people will always want some permanent form of printed matter that gives them the whole story."[56] And Fowler's claim is reinforced by those who point out that videotex receivers allow for only one user at a time and thus can lead to family conflict over what information is to be sought when, whereas the newspaper can be divided into separate sections and read by several persons simultaneously. Of course, if two-, three-, and four-TV set families are the wave of the future, this problem of family stress may not become a major one, at least not with teletext systems.

---

[53] *Ibid.*, p. 28.

[54] "More on Magazines in the '80s," *Magazine Newsletter of Advertising*, 10 (May 1981), p. 1.

[55] *Ibid.*

[56] Quoted in Ray Chapman, "The State of Fleet Street," *The Quill: Magazine for Journalists*, 69 (May 1981), p. 24.

In addition to costs to the user of teletext and viewdata systems, there is also the argument that the costs of manufacturing and the availability of certain components, especially the "ubiquitous electronic chip," will seriously retard the growth of teletext and viewdata systems. As *The* (London) *Economist* put it in March 1980:

> Since 1960 the semiconductor industry has each year doubled the number of transistors or logic functions on a chip, and cut the price of each function by 28%. The average price of a transistor in 1960 was about $10. Now it is less than one cent. This tumbling cost is why electronics fans talk about an approaching era of 'free' intelligence in which computer power can be introduced into almost any product for practically nothing. Would that it were that simple.
>
> The semiconductor industry can no longer keep up with expanding demand. The capital equipment needed to make today's chips is so expensive that, despite increases in capital spending of 50% in 1978 and again in 1979 (so that capital investment now represents 16% of total sales), the top ten American semiconductor manufacturers have been reporting waiting lists of up to ten months.[57]

The Economist contends that the semiconductor industry "is not earning enough profit to finance its own phenomenal growth," that over the past five years, "the industry has suffered a 31% fall in its average return on equity funds and an 18% decline in pretax profits margins," and that capital financiers are now avoiding this industry.[58] The magazine further argues that "the cost of producing software for an application has risen perhaps tenfold," illustrating, "the constraints that software imposes on the spread of supposedly 'free' intelligence."[59]

Summing up its appraisal, *The Economist* states:

> The idea that a marriage of micro-electronics and telecommunications will produce a revolution, exists largely in the imagination—for the moment. It awaits the widespread use of electronic funds transfer, electronic mail and publishing, armchair shopping, remote control of plant and machinery—and, most dramatic of all in its effect on work—the paperless, minimally staffed office of the future.[60]

In short, these are the major arguments against teletext and viewdata: little real evidence of a public need for these new media, a tendency to further isolate people from each other in their "all-electronic caves," superficial treatment of complex issues and serious news, support of the existing political-economic power structures, a dampening of incidental learning about important issues of the day, an increase in family stress, a diluting of the economic resources devoted to serious news-gathering, relatively high

---

[57]Quoted in John Coleman, "Societal implications and the human factor," *Inside Videotex*, p. 117.

[58]*Ibid.*

[59]*Ibid.*

[60]*Ibid.*

cost to the user, lack of portability, difficulty of reading from a television screen, and relatively high cost of manufacturing.

THE EXPERIENCED VIEW

Even though teletext and viewdata systems are in their infancy in most countries except the United Kingdom, some lessons are being learned from operating and experimental systems, and from studies of these systems and their audiences. In this section, I review what we know now from many of the publicly available reports and studies.

1. The editorial aspects of teletext, and especially viewdata, are proving more complex than intially expected. It is not a matter of simply transferring the content of existing printed media to the television screen.[61]

Many of those who have had experience with or studied videotex systems are beginning to conclude that because a videotex screen has only 2–3% of the capacity of a newspaper page at most, and because people seem to be reluctant to read much beyond one screenful for any given story, this implies "a different treatment that excludes most of the comments and analyses that may be legitimately expected from a newspaper."[62] The publisher of the *Yuma Daily Sun,* in describing its cable news service, put it this way:

> News and information is updated hourly until press time, then a full update. All pages on the system are changed an average of three to four times each day. Sun Cable local news does not have the capacity for detail that the paper holds, so we offer only the basic facts of the story in order to create interest for the intimate details found in the afternoon paper. In a story of major importance, we will not "scoop" ourselves on Sun Cable but "break" the story after the press run starts.[63]

In a study of the first two years of the Prestel system in England, Rex Winsbury estimated that "three-quarters of the material on Prestel comes from outside the traditional publishing industry."[64] He also concluded that "editing for Prestel is not like newspaper editing, and not like computer programming, but a novel and challenging mixture of disciplines drawn from both."[65] Winsbury contends that "videotex . . . is not the prerogative

---

[61] Michael Tyler, "Videotex, Prestel and Teletext: The Economics and Politics of Some Electronic Publishing Media," *Telecommunications Policy,* March 1979, p. 44.

[62] Gérard Eymery, "Teletext in France: Antiope-Services," *European Broadcasting Union Review,* 32 (March 1981), p. 54.

[63] Donald N. Soldwedel, "Opportunities for Small Newspapers," *VIDEOTEX '81,* p. 227.

[64] Rex Winsbury, *The Electronic Bookstall: Push-Button Publishing on Videotex* (London: International Institute of Communications, 1979), p. 19.

[65] *Ibid.,* p. 31.

of traditional publishers, or even a subset of them" because a publisher on videotex may be anyone who possesses information that might be of interest or value to others.[66] He argues that the publishers on Prestel tend to be those who offer specialist information, not the general newspapers that cover the widest possible variety of topics to catch the largest and widest possible audience.

In discussing the kinds of information that Prestel is best suited to carry, Winsbury cites financial data, classified advertising, and other "directory" information—anything that is a list, guide, or table, such as addresses, sports results, houses for sale, retail prices, cinema showings, or train times. As he puts it, "It is less clear whether Prestel is suitable for discussion, analysis, extended description, or a long newspaper story."[67] Winsbury thinks it is "a total mistake to regard videotex as some sort of 'electronic clone' of the newspaper," because this attitude produces, "stiff, dull pages that do not exploit the characteristics of videotex and, in a broader sense, narrows the mind about what can be done and said in the new medium."[68] He cautions newspapers, however, not to ignore videotex because of the inroads it may make into classified advertising revenues and into readers of sports and entertainment information.

Another very important point made by Winsbury is that "the idea of a social and political role is central to newspapers, foreign to computers," and it is not clear at this time that either teletext or viewdata systems will be any more than storehouses of, "rather neutral reference information (typically, train and airline timetables, cinema listings, economic statistics) of a relatively static nature and little, if any, controversial content."[69] This point was echoed recently by Philip Meyer of Knight-Ridder Newspapers when he argued before the Videotex '81 conference in Toronto that "information . . . does not fully define what newspapers do."[70] Meyer contends that by making itself, "a credible, heeded, respected voice in the community," the newspaper can deliver "influence along with the information," and thus both information and the context of information.[71] He questions whether videotex systems can deliver such influence and context along with specialized information, arguing, "Prestel's role is more that of a neutral broker of information than maintainer of community beliefs and values."[72] Meyer disagrees somewhat with those who argue that videotex systems

---

[66]*Ibid.*, p. 57.
[67]*Ibid.*, p. 61.
[68]*Ibid.*, pp. 61–62.
[69]*Ibid.*, p. 67.
[70]Philip Meyer, "Emerging Opportunities in Electronic Technology: What Can We Learn from Newspapers," *VIDEOTEX '81*, p. 233.
[71]*Ibid.*
[72]*Ibid.*, p. 234.

are capable of delivering only very short news and information items when he points out that reporters from Knight-Ridder's experimental Viewtron system in Coral Gables, Florida, found, "they could deliver local news with greater speed and in more detail than *The Miami Herald*'s semi-weekly zoned section for the area of the country which includes Coral Gables."[73] And he notes that contrary to the reported Prestel experience, they (users) had the patience to read long stories, dutifully pushing the button to turn the pages a dozen times or more."[74] Meyer's experience with longer stories on Viewtron is contrary to the experience with all other teletext and viewdata systems included in this study, and even Meyer acknowledges that newspaper companies experimenting with Prestel are "beginning to find that it is easier to clear the market with small packages of information, frequently updated, aimed at highly specialized segments . . . more readily found in the business community."[75]

This view is supported by a recent study in the Federal Republic of Germany that concludes that viewdata systems are especially good for short, timely news items, sports results, and short political announcements that can be easily updated.[76] Likewise, a review of viewdata and teletext in the United States by George Alexander of *The Seybold Report* (an authoritative newsletter dealing with electronics in publishing) concludes such systems, "are not suited to lengthy text presentations, and their graphics are more like diagrams than photos."[77]

2. Some patterns of use of teletext and viewdata systems are beginning to emerge, suggesting that these media are less suited to browsing than are print media and more suited to the seeking of specific, short items of information than longer analyses and extended discussions.

It is becoming increasingly apparent that just as it is not possible simply to transfer the content of printed media to the television screen, it is also not possible to read words on the TV screen in the same manner that one reads words from the printed page. In a recent study of 125 receivers of a teletext service offered through a subscription TV system near Miami, Florida, Oak Communications found that those who had used their teletext system from 1–3 months were critical of the limited content of a page (about 80 words) especially where one article was continued through several pages. Users also indicated that the information was "choppy," and they were "especially

---

[73]*Ibid.*, p. 235.

[74]*Ibid.*, pp. 235–36.

[75]*Ibid.*, p. 235.

[76]Forschungsgruppe Kammerer: *Struktur, Spektrum und Potentiale der geschäftlichen Bildschirmtext-nutzung* (Köln, 1981).

[77]George Alexander, "Viewdata and Teletext: New Electronic Home Information Delivery Systems," *The Seybold Report*, 10 (November 24, 1980), p. 14.

critical" of the page access time, which could run as long as 30 seconds.[78]
Charles Eissler of Oak Communications concluded from this study that
although the informational content of the teletext system "is the main product," much of the perceived value of such a system, "is the appearance
and operating convenience of the hardware."[79]

More to the point regarding information seeking patterns of users, a recent survey of 609 teletext users in the United Kingdom by Philips Electronics shows that in a typical week, the average teletext user makes use of
the service 77 times but spends not quite two hours watching teletext
pages.[80] Richard Hooper, director of Prestel, notes that the average use of
that service per day is 9 minutes.[81] Both of these findings suggest that
teletext and viewdata are "in-and-out" media that are more suited to the
presentation of short, specific items than to more lengthy articles that require extended periods of concentration by the reader.

A 1980 survey of 227 users of teletext (from an estimated 70,000 receivers
in private homes) in the Netherlands indicates that 63% of those whose
prime interest was in reading news pages used teletext mainly for the most
recent news of the last couple of hours.[82] But 75% of those reading the news
section leafed through other pages besides those where they expected interesting news, suggesting some browsing in the news section. This was not
true, however, in the broadcasting section (information about television
and radio programs) where 74% claimed to read only those pages where interesting news was expected. It must be remembered, however, than even
where browsing did occur, most of the news stories were very short—usually not more than one page (80 words or so) in length. Still, this study suggests that people may be willing to browse through some kinds of material
on videotex systems if the individual items are not lengthy.

Browsing on teletext and viewdata systems is not as easy as with printed
matter, however, primarily because of the limited word capacity of the
television screen and the necessity to press a specific number to get another
page. One experiment in England at the Loughborough University of
Technology has suggested that although the "menu" (index) approach on

---

[78]Charles O. Eissler, "Market Testing Video-text: Oak's Miami Teletext System,"
VIDEOTEX '81, p. 69.

[79]*Ibid.*

[80]Philips Teletext Users' Survey (London: Philips Video Division, 1981).

[81]Richard Hooper, "The UK Scene—Teletext and Videotex," *VIDEOTEX '81*, p. 133.

[82]Netherlands Broadcasting Foundation Teletext Survey (Hilversum: NOS, 1981). These
data were generously supplied by Dr. Harold de Bock, director of the Audience Research
Service of NOS.

[83]T. Stewart, "PRESTEL—How Usable Is It?" in Eberhard Witte, ed., *Human Aspects of
Telecommunication* (New York: Springer-Verlag, 1980), pp. 116–17.

Prestel is fairly easy to use, it "can be made faster and use fewer pages if it is supplemented with a printed directory."[83] The results of this study also suggest that people could find specific information more quickly and easily if "a limited keyword facility" was provided where users could enter simple words instead of page numbers.

3. The expenditures for teletext and viewdata services by the general public for home use have been very modest so far, and they are likely to remain so in the foreseeable future.

There is evidence that despite the recent development of many communications devices, "the share of information goods and services in household expenditure remains modest."[84] There is also data to suggest that the proportion of household income devoted to communication media has remained rather constant over the past 40 years or so.[85] Tyler writes that in 1976 the average British household spent about £4 a month on printed media, about £3½ on telecommunications and postage, about £6 on television and radio receivers and license fees, and about £2½ on tickets to cinemas, theaters, and sporting events. He argues that if a videotex service could be offered for, say, £12 a month for terminal rental and usage charges, the money for such a service would "imply a considerable diversion of expenditure from other information-related items in the household budget; *or,* if the diversions hypothesized are to be kept within reasonable limits, we must assume some diversion of other kinds of discretionary expenditures (say, luxury clothing or leisure automobile trips) in favour of Videotex."[86]

In a more recent article based on quantitative models of videotex markets developed by Communication Studies and Planning International (CSP), Tyler writes that although there is evidence emerging for a mass residential market for electronic publishing and transaction services, "the levels of expenditure per household associated with substantial market penetration—say 25% or more of households—are likely to be low—of the order of $5-10 per month, depending on the range of services offered."[87] He claims, however, that there are limited market segments, such as hobbyists or professional and business people working from home, that will pay much more. And Tyler thinks, "While videotex has some limitations as an advertising medium, it is highly cost-effective for classified advertising and many classes of transactions."[88]

[83]Tyler, "Videotex, Prestel and Teletext," p. 46.

[84]Maxwell E. McCombs, "Mass Media in the Marketplace," *Journalism Monographs,* 24 (August 1972).

[86]Tyler, *op. cit.,* p. 47.

[87]Michael Tyler and Paige Amidon, "Prospects for Videotex: An Independent Perspective," *VIDEOTEX '81,* p. 469.

[88]*Ibid.*

A report from a British government-organized private conference on a national commitment to teletext and viewdata in January 1981, reinforces Tyler's view that people are not likely to pay much for the use of teletext and viewdata systems in their homes. The report concludes that teletext systems in Britain are "too expensive" at £3–£5 above the regular monthly rental price of an ordinary television set, and argues that "with a rental premium of £1 per month and a retail premium between £30–£50 Teletext would become a standard feature not only for the replacement market, but also for second sets and first time purchases."[89] The report maintains that cost is a problem for widespread teletext diffusion, "but certainly not an intractable one."[90]

With regard to the Prestel viewdata system, the report admonishes that "the same unfortunately cannot be said for Prestel,"[91] implying that cost may indeed be an unsolvable obstacle to the widespread diffusion of Prestel in the domestic home market. As the report puts it, "There is still no real evidence that there will ever be a mass residential market for Prestel."[92] This conslusion is elaborated on by "information to hand" that suggests that interest in Prestel "only starts when the rental premium falls to £10 per month" (it was £15 at the time of the conference). The report also states that "at a premium of £7 per month (£200 retail) one third of the potential users would be interested; and only when the premium falls to £4 per month (£120 retail) does significant interest ensue, i.e., four out of five people."[93] As for maintenance of a Prestel receiver, "£1 per week running costs seems to be an acceptable figure."[94] Whether or not costs can be brought down to these levels is questionable because, as the report puts it, "We are now faced with a chicken and egg situation where costs cannot come down significantly until set sales and usage increases (sic), which they won't do until costs come down, etc., etc."[95]

In the United States, a study by Oak Communications of its experimental teletext system near Miami, Florida, suggests that about three fourths of approximately 125 users would be willing to pay for a teletext service, but only between $5–$25 per month.[96] Edgar Gladstone, who directed a study of consumer entertainment and information systems for Quantum Science Corporation, states that one of the major conclusions of the study was that

---

[89]"Teletext & Viewdata: The Commitment Conference" (London: Department of Industry and National Economic Development Office, 1981), p. 1–3.

[90]*Ibid.*

[91]*Ibid.*

[92]*Ibid.*, p. 1–4.

[93]*Ibid.*

[94]*Ibid.*

[95]*Ibid.*, p. 1–5.

[96]Eissler, "Market Testing Video-text," *VIDEOTEX '81*, p. 69.

such systems "must provide a package of free and paid-for information" and that "in the end, shopping from home and other transactions will be the real economic justification for home-information services" because profits from those activities will justify offering free services to get people to buy sets with decoders.[97]

Thus, the evidence to date suggests that most people are not likely to pay much beyond a few dollars per month for teletext and viewdata services in their homes. This may be because, as one study concluded, "People are accustomed to paying for entertainment, but not for using the library."[98] Unless videotex services offer features in addition to information, such as shopping from home, electronic banking, etc., most people are not likely to pay much for them.

4. In addition to cost, other factors such as awareness, ease of use, and perceived utility suggest a mass market for teletext systems and a largely business or elite market for viewdata systems, at least in the near future.

According to Brian Champness of Plymouth Polytechnic in England, recent studies of teletext and viewdata use in homes in the United Kingdom suggest that teletext, "has a good chance of taking off, but that there will only be a residential market for Prestel if it becomes as cheap as teletext."[99] There is also some indication from these studies that viewers don't see the need for the nearly 200,000 pages of information provided by Prestel on their televisions. This conclusion is supported by a follow-up report from the recent Teletext and Viewdata Commitment Conference in London, which states:

> The active, aggressive, and immediate promotion of Teletext in the consumer marketplace, along with Prestel's carefully targetted marketing programme at the business community, will be the best way to accelerate the arrival of mass market Viewdata, as well as consolidate the growth of Teletext.[100]

A large study of electronic information systems by Arthur D. Little, Inc. in the United States suggests that teletext is something that would be of mass appeal, "reaching an unlimited number of people instantaneously and all at the same time," whereas viewdata "will inevitably interest wealthier and more educated people who will be willing to pay for the convenience offered by the system."[101] Another study of the communication behavior of

---

[97] Scott R. Schmedel, "TV Systems Enabling Viewers to Call Up Printed Data Catch Eye of Media Firms," *The Wall Street Journal,* July 24, 1979, p. 40.

[98] Joseph N. Pelton, "The Future of Telecommunications: A Delphi Survey," *Journal of Communication,* 31 (Winter 1981), p. 181.

[99] Brian Champness, "Social Uses of Videotex and Teletext in UK," *VIDEOTEX '81,* p. 333.

[100] "Teletext & Viewdata: The Commitment Conference" (From Commitment to Action, p. 1).

[101] Kelly, "All The News," p. 17.

1000 persons in two communities in England by the Centre for Mass Communication Research at the University of Leicester arrives at much the same conclusion: "Examining the specific case of Prestel . . . there can be little doubt that members of the higher socio-economic group are likely to be the early adopters."[102]

The conclusion that a viewdata system such as Prestel should appeal more to the up-scale business market than to the mass domestic should come as no surprise when one considers that the information providers, or publishers, on Prestel "are, foremost, the companies who can offer specialist information."[103] If Prestel and other viewdata systems like it are intended to serve a domestic as well as a business market and are to be used by all manner of people, the Leicester study concludes:

> The data base must be truly comprehensive and the information must be presented in a clear and simple manner. Moreover, the data base must include information on all the many topics about which information is required by different groups of people to enable them to cope with their everyday problems and to help them advance their interests and improve their quality of life. This means that a large number of topics will have to be covered, and our research clearly shows that much of the required information is likely to be highly specific, quite detailed, and often local in emphasis.[104]

The study also argues that "the common carrier policy of British Telecom suggests that if the present policy is maintained, it is unlikely that such a comprehensive service will be provided," and "much more planning, direction, and attention to identified needs will be necessary before effective community and recreation information packages can be carried on the service, and before an acceptable proportion of the general public can be persuaded that the adoption of Prestel would be worthwhile."[105]

In addition to these views from the United Kingdom and the United States, a 1980 study of the structure, scope, and potential of the commercial use of viewdata in the Federal Republic of Germany suggests that the system can be used by commercial enterprises for internal communication, distribution of goods and services, and service to customers, as well as for information and entertainment.[106] The study argues that viewdata is especially well suited to mail order businesses, advertisers, and public institutions.

5. Both teletext and viewdata systems probably will not do much to nar-

---

[102]Peggy Gray, "A Study of Communication Behaviour" (Leicester: Centre for Mass Communication Research, University of Leicester, 1981), pp. 103–04.

[103]Winsbury, *The Electronic Bookstall,* p. 56.

[104]Gray, "A Study of Communication Behaviour," pp. 102–03.

[105]*Ibid.,* p. 103.

[106]Forschungsgruppe Kammerer: *Struktur, Spektrum und Potentiale der geschäftlichen Bildschirmtext-nutzung* (Köln, 1981).

row the knowledge gap between lower and higher socio-economic groups. In fact, they may widen this gap.

Although this conclusion is more speculative than the previous four, it is somewhat consistent with them. Considering the very limited word capacity of a videotex screen, the evidence that both teletext and viewdata systems are more suited to the seeking of specific, short items than to the reading of longer analyses and extended discussions, the relatively high cost of teletext and especially viewdata, and the likelihood that viewdata systems such as Prestel will succeed in the business rather than residential market, it is not unreasonable to suspect that these systems will do little to narrow the knowledge gap between the information rich and the information poor.

Although teletext systems such as Ceefax and Oracle do stand a reasonable chance of becoming truly mass media, they are not likely to provide the kind of information needed by many less well-off people to improve their standard of living. The Leicester study of communication behavior in two English cities found that most people needed knowledge about housing, entertainment, travel, taxation, consumer problems, education, pension matters, and welfare questions.[107] And, as mentioned earlier, the study suggested that the required information should be "highly specific, quite detailed, and often local in emphasis."[108] While the teletext systems in the United Kingdom do provide facts about entertainment and travel, they generally provide none about housing, taxation, consumer problems, education, pension matters, and welfare questions. Even the information concerning entertainment and travel is not usually highly specific and local, and it is not likely to be so in the future unless some way is found to increase greatly the number of pages devoted to regional and local data. As it stands now, Ceefax and Oracle are national teletext systems, not regional or local.

The Prestel viewdata system, on the other hand, does have the page capacity (currently about 200,000) to enable it to carry highly specific, local facts on a wide variety of subjects, but at present Prestel concentrates mainly on information of interest to businesses and commercial organizations, and its chances of becoming a mass domestic medium are highly questionable, especially if it continues to emphasize business and commercial material. As the Leicester study put it, with regard to the specific case of Prestel:

> It is unlikely that "communication needs of society" will figure prominently in our deliberations if the economics of the market place are allowed to prevail. So, granted these circumstances, the use of Prestel in the immediate future is not likely to do much to close the gap between the information rich and the information poor.[109]

---

[107]Gray, "A Study of Communication Behaviour," pp. 94–95.

[108]*Ibid.,* pp. 102–03.

[109]*Ibid.,* p. 108.

Whether this conclusion applies to teletext and viewdata systems outside the United Kingdom, or whether it will hold for those systems in England in the future, remains to be seen. It may indeed be overly pessimistic at this early stage to argue that teletext and viewdata will not do much to reduce the information gap between lower and higher socio-economic groups. But the lessons learned from experience with and research on videotex systems so far are not overly encouraging.

6. The impact of teletext and viewdata systems on existing communication media has been almost negligible thus far, and the future impact seems to depend on many factors such as cost, legibility, investment by other organizations, ease of use, promotion, and perceived utility.

Although there was much concern among many print-publishing organizations, especially newspapers, when Ceefax and Oracle were introduced in the United Kingdom in the mid-1970s, this anxiety has lessened in recent years, probably because of the lack of advertising on these teletext systems and probably because of the slow growth of the Prestel viewdata system. However, as Michael Tyler notes, "The interests of the print media as such *may* be threatened by competition from new media."[110] Tyler, like others, argues that the kinds of print media particularly at risk are specialized magazines and local newspapers—both highly dependent upon classified advertising in the United Kingdom.

Even though it may be true that those printed media most dependent upon classified advertising may be most vulnerable to economic undermining by teletext and viewdata systems, it is not at all clear when this might happen. A previously mentioned study of electronic information systems by the consulting firm of Arthur D. Little, Inc., concluded that "the electronic services will not be a major threat to newspapers in the next 15 years, the time frame of our study."[111] Donald Sparrow, director of the study, cautions, however, "Beyond 1992 there could be a more severe impact."[112] Another study of electronic information systems conducted by Quantum Science Corporation suggested that one of the major uses of such systems would be advertising and purchasing products and services. Edgar Gladstone, director of consumer studies at Quantum Science, said, "I see it impacting advertising quite a bit."[113] He believes the big newspapers will try to get into the electronic information delivery market first to protect their advertising revenues, and he concludes, "There's going to be a pretty strong impact on newspapers."[114]

---

[110]Tyler, "Videotex, Prestel, and Teletext," p. 48.
[111]Quoted in Kelly, "All The News," p. 16.
[112]*Ibid.*
[113]*Ibid.,* p. 17.
[114]*Ibid.*

Rex Winsbury, in his 1979 study of the Prestel system in England, maintains, "It will take a long time for the effect of videotex systems to be felt on newspapers."[115] He argues that when it comes, the effect will be "patchy"—felt in some areas but not in others—and that such effects, "Will not spell the doom of the newspaper but add to the pressures for further modification of its role in the electronic era."[116] This view is echoed by Benjamin Compaine in his study of the U.S. newspaper industry, in which he concludes that economic considerations will preclude any major development of the electronic newspaper in the foreseeable future, even though there may be a market for electronic distribution of supplemental news and information to businesses.[117] Compaine believes that display advertising in newspapers is fairly secure but that classified advertising does lend itself to potential new forms of delivery. Yet, he argues, "The form of the newspaper by the year 2000 should be remarkably similar to the newspaper of 1980," and "the paper may be thinner as certain sections may be replaced by electronic distribution."[118]

Robert Johnson, vice president and general manager of *The Columbus (Ohio) Dispatch,* writes that since *The Dispatch* began to be delivered electronically to home video terminals via the CompuServe system in July 1980, the management has concluded that "electronic publishing of the daily paper is not of significant value in the local market—we are in competition with ourselves at a much higher price for a less complete product."[119] Johnson also asserts that *The Dispatch* "will always include a substantial portion of our daily paper in the (CompuServe) data base because it costs next to nothing to provide, and the preliminary evidence shows it is of substantial interest outside our circulation area."[120]

As for classified advertising, it seems from *The Dispatch* experiment that programming such advertising is more complicated than programming news for the computer. Gary Wilson of *The Dispatch* explains that whereas news is on the system for a 24–hour cycle and then replaced, classified can be on one day, two days, a week, or until forbidden. Wilson also notes that the indexing becomes difficult: "If you are looking for a Chevrolet, and a Ford dealer has a used one, it has to be a complex program to handle all of the possibilities."[121] At any one time, according to Wilson, *The Dispatch* can

[115]Winsbury, *The Electronic Bookstall,* p. 54.

[116]*Ibid.*

[117]Benjamin M. Compaine, *The Newspaper Industry in the 1980s: An Assessment of Economics and Technology* (White Plains, N.Y.: Knowledge Industry Publications, 1980).

[118]*Ibid.,* pp. 222–23.

[119]Robert M. Johnson, "Electronic News Delivery—The Dispatch/CompuServe Experiment," *VIDEOTEX '81,* p. 240.

[120]*Ibid.,* p. 241.

[121]Quoted in Ray Laakaniemi, "The Computer Connection: America's First Computer–Delivered Newspaper," *Newspaper Research Journal,* 2 (July 1981), p. 67.

have up to 10,000 classified ads in its system, making the indexing a very difficult programming assignment.

In spite of the difficulties involved in the programming of classified advertising, there is evidence to suggest that, as Philip Meyer, formerly of Knight-Ridder Newspapers, puts it, "The main threat to newspapers is not competition for information, but competition for advertising."[122] Even though Winsbury, in his study of Prestel, argues that it will take a long time for videotex systems to affect newspapers, he also concludes that viewdata systems such as Prestel will be good at delivering financial information, classified advertisements, and "routine information" such as sports scores and statistics, weather forecasts, entertainment guides, births, and deaths, and "anything that is a list or guide or table."[123]

In order for videotex systems to take classified advertising away from newspapers and specialist magazines, however, there must be widespread penetration of the communities served by these newspapers and magazines. In other words, videotex systems must be accepted by most of the people now being reached by various newspaper and magazines. Considering the other lessons learned from experience and research, widespread acceptance seems to be dependent upon legibility and ease of use, low cost, ready availability, perceived need, and a change in the way people regard the television—from primarily an entertainment medium to a sometime provider of information. As Winsbury puts it, "The TV screen was not designed for reading but for TV movies."[124] And, as he points out, the cost, availability, ease of use, and content of videotex systems will depend heavily on the scale of investment by the public telephone and telecommunication authorities, TV set manufacturers, information providers, software and system designers, and other parties.[125]

All of these factors suggest one central question—how fast will teletext and viewdata systems be accepted? Or, to put it in Winsbury's words, how fast will these systems become "user-friendly"?[126]

7. Although it is impossible to study the future empirically, the estimates based on present studies suggest that the adoption of viewdata systems in industrialized countries is likely to happen rather slowly as compared to the adoption rate of television.

A recent Delphi study of "some 150 experts around the world" by Joseph Pelton finds that about 84% of those responding to the survey believed that

[122]*Ibid.*

[123]Winsbury, *The Electronic Bookstall,* pp. 59–61.

[124]*Ibid.,* p. 55.

[125]*Ibid.,* p. 54.

[126]*Ibid.,* p. 55.

viewdata would be in use in 5-10% of homes in the O.E.C.D. (Organization for Economic Cooperation and Development) countries by 1985 to 2000.[127] Pelton points out that even though various market studies have predicted that the more sophisticated viewdata systems such as Prestel, Antiope, and Telidon can be expected to grow rapidly in the O.E.C.D. countries in the next few years, there are a number of inhibiting factors such as the level of sophistication required of the user, the costs to the user, the kind of information or services the user will pay for, and the fact that viewdata systems are in competition with other systems already delivering information electronically (computerized data bases, specialized mail services, and cable TV systems). Pelton concludes that if the Delphi experts are correct, "it will be some time before a significant portion of the public (that is, more than 10%) acquires the viewdata habit."[128]

A review of recent studies of teletext and viewdata use in homes by Brian Champness of Plymouth Polytechnic in England "provides some comfort for CEEFAX and ORACLE providers, but little joy for those who believe that the information revolution is around the corner."[129] Champness argues that the impact of both viewdata and teletext in the United Kingdom on the population at large "can better be described as a gentle evolution rather than a technological revolution. Current evidence suggests that it will stay that way."[130] A recent study of the commercial use of viewdata in the Federal Republic of Germany, drawing on a nationwide sample of 220 experts, finds that viewdata is not a basic innovation and that its acceptance will happen rather slowly, more like the acceptance of the telephone than the television.[131]

Efrem Sigel, editor in chief of Knowledge Industry Publications and first author of a recent book on videotex, writes, "It is well to understand that none of the videotext systems discussed in this book will necessarily succeed on a large scale."[132] Siegel identifies four "natural obstacles" to the growth of teletext (use of TV for entertainment, difficulty of reading from a TV screen, lack of portability of a TV set, and low cost of newspapers and magazines), and argues that many of these same problems face viewdata systems. He also sees additional problems for viewdata systems, including the high cost of specially-equipped TV sets, the "bewildering profusion" of information on such systems that contributes to lack of focused marketing

---

[127]Pelton, "The Future of Telecommunications," p. 180.

[128]*Ibid.,* p. 182.

[129]Champness, "Social Uses of Videotex and Teletext," pp. 332–33.

[130]*Ibid.,* p. 339.

[131]Forschungsgruppe Kammerer: *Struktur, Spektrum und Potentiale der geschäftlichen Bildschirmtext-nutzung* (Köln, 1981).

[132]Efrem Sigel, *Videotext: The Coming Revolution in Home/Office Information Retrieval* (White Plains, N.Y.: Knowledge Industry Publications, 1980), p. 129.

efforts, and the resulting lack of a clear identity for such systems in comparison with printed publications. Sigel does see "undeniable promise" in both teletext and viewdata systems, but he believes that the changes they entail in the established ways of doing things "are so profound that they will never take place in a period of months, or even in a year or two."[133]

Even in the United Kingdom, where teletext and viewdata systems were first begun on a regular operating basis, the projections for the future growth of teletext and viewdata imply rather slow acceptance. The 1981 Teletext and Viewdata Commitment Conference report suggests 300,000 teletext TV set sales in 1981, 700,000 in 1982 and 1.2 million in 1983.[134] These projected sales, limited as they are in comparison to the 19 million or so licensed TV sets in the United Kingdom, stand in sharp contrast to the track record so far—113,000 teletext sets and 7000 adaptors sold between 1977 and the end of 1980.[135] This record also compares poorly with about 1.3 milllion color TV sets sold in the first four years after introduction in 1968.[136]

The conference report also suggests a goal of 50,000 business Prestel set/adaptor installations in the next 18 months (by July of 1982), and 1 million Prestel users by the end of 1985.[137] Again, these projections stand in marked contrast to the nearly 11,000 viewdata sets and adaptors sold in 1979 and 1980,[138] and to the nearly 200,000 color TV sets sold in the first two years of availability.[139]

Thus, these figures from the Commitment Conference report suggest that teletext sets, and especially viewdata sets, will not diffuse nearly as rapidly throughout the United Kingdom as did color television after its introduction in 1968. There is no guarantee that either teletext or viewdata sets will achieve the same overall widespread penetration that color television has, either in the United Kingdom or in other countries.

> But, as Sigel points out:
> Since the U.S. has by far the largest number of computers, computer terminals, telephones and TV sets of any country in the world, it seems safe to make the following prediction: if videotext is viable at all, it will spread wider and faster in the U.S. than elsewhere, even if it comes two or three years later.[140]

---

[133]*Ibid.*, p. 134.
[134]"Teletext & Viewdata: The Commitment Conference," p. 1–8.
[135]*Ibid.*, pp. 1–9 and 10–2.
[136]*Ibid.*, p. 3–3.
[137]*Ibid.*, p. 1–8.
[138]*Ibid.*, p. 1–9.
[139]*Ibid.*, p. 3–3.
[140]Sigel, *Videotext*, p. 8.

SUMMING UP

In this chapter, I have reviewed the major arguments for and against teletext and viewdata systems, and attempted to isolate seven major lessons learned from experience with and research concerning these systems. It should be clear to the reader by now that much of the writing and discussion of videotex as a medium is highly speculative because of its very early stages of development and because of the concerns over its future impact on other media and on the society at large. Only time will tell whether the optimists are more or less correct than the pessimists, and what effects teletext and viewdata will have on the existing media order and on other aspects of our societies.

Another point to be remembered is that the findings summarized in the seven lessons presented in this chapter are based on present uses and technology of teletext and viewdata systems. The technology is certain to change in various ways in the coming years (the resolution of characters on the screen will be made much sharper, the screen size may be expanded, the access time for particular pages will be cut considerably, etc.) and these changes may mean dramatic shifts in the content and uses of these systems. If such shifts in functions do occur, these lessons learned may seem curiously outdated and shortsighted in years to come. Yet, if teletext and viewdata systems continue to develop in the shadow of older media, and are designed to take over many of the functions of these older media without substantially changing these functions, then these lessons may stand the test of time rather well.

3 The Present Study

As noted in Chapter 1, this study focuses on the impact of videotex technology on journalists and their work, on the flow of news and information in society, and on other media. In doing so, it breaks with most of the other electronic information delivery research presently being done, which tends to concentrate on the technological and marketing aspects of this technology, rather than its journalistic implications.

QUESTIONS

To gather information on the effects teletext and viewdata systems are presently having on journalists and their work, I reviewed several studies of journalists in the United States and Britain, including Jeremy Tunstall's study of 200 specialist correspondents in England,[1] John Johnstone et al.'s (1971) study of 1300 practicing journalists in the United States,[2] and an ongoing study of 400 British journalists being conducted by Philip Elliott of the University of Leicester.[3] From these studies I constructed a question-

---

[1] Jeremy Tunstall, *Journalists at Work* (London: Constable, 1971). Also published by Sage Publications, Beverly Hills, California, in 1971.

[2] John Johnstone, Edward Slawski, & William Bowman, *The News People* (Urbana: University of Illinois Press, 1976).

[3] Personal communication and consultation with Philip Elliott, Centre for Mass Communication Research, University of Leicester, England, February 25 and 26, 1981, and May 5, 1981.

naire for teletext and viewdata journalists that included measures of previous employment, job activities, perceptions of adequacy of news sources, necessary job skills, professional attitudes, future intentions, perceptions of audiences, appropriateness of various reporting methods, and other items. (See Appendix 3 for a copy of this questionnaire.) I also composed the following questions to guide my in-depth interviews with journalists working for teletext and viewdata organizations:

1. What are the chief *differences* between working as a journalist for an electronic news delivery system such as Ceefax or Oracle and working for a more conventional broadcast or print news organization?

2. What proportion of time, in an average week, is spent on reporting (gathering information), editing, administrative work,and other duties in an electronic news delivery organization as compared to a more conventional news organization? How much "active" versus "passive" (rewriting, rekeyboarding) newsgathering is going on in each setting? Do you expect this pattern to continue in the future?

3. How much *autonomy,* or freedom, do you have in selecting and writing news stories for electronic delivery as compared to selecting and writing news stories for broadcast or print?

4. How much *feedback* on the quality of work is provided (in terms of editors' comments, readership studies, letters, etc.) in an electronic news delivery setting? In a more conventional television, newspaper, or news magazine setting? Are you satisfied with this amount of feedback? Would you like more, less, or what?

5. If you have a good idea for a subject which you think should be reported, how often are you able to get the subject covered in an electronic news delivery setting? (Almost always, more often than not, only occasionally, never) In a television newsroom? In a newspaper newsroom? In a news magazine setting?

6. What aspects of electronic news delivery work do you particularly like? Which aspects of such work do you particularly dislike?

7. How often are news stories usually updated on your electronic news delivery system? Do you think they should be updated less often, more often, or about as often as they are now? Does updating pose any problems for you that you would not have in a more conventional broadcast or print journalism setting?

8. Is it true that persons working for electronic delivery systems such as Ceefax and Oracle tend to be younger and relatively inexperienced as journalists? Are there opportunities for advancement in position and pay? Are electronic news delivery jobs regarded as pretty much "dead-end"?

To assess media executives' and journalists' perceptions of the impact of videotex systems on the flow of news in society, I devised the following questions to guide my in-depth interviews:

1. "What is changing is the delivery system of the newspaper, not so much the news–gathering process." (Quote from Mark Ethridge III of the Charlotte (N.C.) *Observer* after viewing and using Knight-Ridder Newspapers' Viewtron experiment in Coral Gables, Florida.) Agree? True with existing systems?

2. "But the Viewtron experiment does make it clear that the coming of the electronic newspaper means important changes for the printed newspaper, both in forms and in the way we edit and select stories." (Quote from Mark Ethridge III in APME's "Electronic Publishing" report, November 1980, p. 11) Agree? How will the way journalists edit and select stories change with electronic news delivery? How has it changed with the Ceefax and Oracle systems? With other systems?

3. "Because computer memory space is cheaper than newsprint, stories can run as long as anyone wants them to." (Quote from M. Ethridge III) Agree? Is this true with existing systems?

4. Is there a need for more powerful, punchier leads in the first 100 words of news stories being written for an electronic delivery system, as opposed to such stories being written for a newspaper or a magazine? For a broadcast news program?

5. Is it true that electronic news delivery systems may have less of an "agenda-setting function" than do more conventional news media? That is, can people select only that information that they think interests them and avoid stumbling across a piece of worthwhile information on a subject they think doesn't interest them?

6. Henry Heilbrunn of Associated Press describes writing for their "Viewdata wire" as somewhere between writing for a broadcast wire and the full wire—more than for radio or television but less than for a newspaper. Is this true with Ceefax, Oracle and other existing systems?

7. Does the perception of what is "newsworthy" for existing electronic news delivery systems hinge mainly on how recent, or *timely,* the events are? Is there much news about trends over time or ongoing processes, as compared to the more conventional broadcast and print media? What topics are considered "good" news stories by electronic news delivery journalists as compared to more conventional print and broadcast journalists?

8. What kinds of *news sources* are relied upon in the electronic news delivery systems as compared to more conventional media? Is more, less, or the same amount of reliance placed upon documentary material, the

telephone, face-to-face interviews with news sources, discussions with other journalists, etc.? Are news stories more likely to involve multiple sources in a more conventional newsroom setting than in an electronic news delivery setting?

9. Are news stories carried on electronic news delivery systems such as Ceefax and Oracle as likely to deal with matters of *public controversy,* where different positions are taken, as are news stories carried in the more conventional print and broadcast media?

10. How much news story overlap is there between electronic news delivery systems and the more conventional printed and broadcast news media? Do BBC staffers share "carbons" with Ceefax journalists? Is the same true for the ITV and Oracle journalists? Does the introduction of electronic news delivery systems result in any more diversity of news? Any less?

11. What is the greatest impact that electronic news delivery has had on the nature of British (Dutch, Belgian, etc.) news?

12. What "myths" about electronic news delivery's impact on news have you encountered, if any?

13. What will electronic news delivery do to news coverage of television, newspapers and news magazines in the next 10 years?

14. If it is true that the teletext and viewdata systems tend to be staffed by younger, less experienced persons on the whole, what does this imply for the *quality* of news reporting on such systems? For the condensing of news information gathered by more experienced journalists?

To try to gauge the likely effects of teletext and viewdata on newsroom organization and on other media, I asked the following questions of media executives and of journalists:

1. How does the introduction of electronic news delivery affect the organization of a broadcast or print newsroom? Is there a need for a separate editor to oversee the operation? A separate desk? Separate reporters? Separate copy editors? Separate typists to rekeyboard material into the electronic delivery system? Separate graphic artists for creating visuals?

2. Does electronic news delivery make it necessary to hire "round-the-clock" editors and reporters to update stories? Are deadlines more frequent than in more conventional newsrooms?

3. What qualities are sought in journalists who are to work for electronic news delivery systems? Are these qualities any different from those desired in newspaper and television journalists? In what way?

4. Is specialization of reporting less, greater, or about the same in an electronic news delivery setting as compared to a more conventional broad-

cast or print newsroom setting? How important is expertise in a certain subject matter for a journalist (reporter or editor) working for an electronic news delivery system?

5. How would you rate development of electronic news delivery (either teletext or viewdata) in your media organization? Is it a high, moderate, or low priority venture? Do the chief executives of the organization consider it very important, somewhat important, or not too important?

6. Has the introduction of electronic news delivery had much impact on the competition for scarce resources in your media organization? Are more expensive, in-depth stories covered less frequently since electronic news was begun? Are there costs to other parts of your organization? Were these costs of electronic news delivery anticipated before it was introduced? Do you think these costs are justified, or will be justified in the future? Why?

7. How do other journalists in your organization view those who work with the electronic news delivery system? Is there much tension between the more conventional journalists and those who work with the electronic news delivery system? If so, how do you think such tension can be reduced?

8. In what ways has electronic news delivery affected your media organization to date? What changes in the organization do you predict will occur in the next five to ten years as a result of electronic news delivery?

9. Do you think electronic delivery systems should be *operated* by media organizations in the future, or should media concentrate on *supplying* certain kinds of information (especially news) to such delivery systems and leave their ownership and management to others?

10. If it's true that there are relatively few experienced journalists working with teletext and viewdata systems, and that such jobs are not high in prestige or pay, what does this imply for the future development of such systems as *news* media? Will such electronic delivery systems continue to be viewed as second-rate by many of the more experienced broadcast and print journalists?

Although these questions guided my in-depth interviews with various media executives and journalists, not all questions were asked of every person and some additional questions were asked as the interviews progressed. However, most of these questions served as the common thread running through these interviews.

METHODS

The findings of this study are based on interviews with key executives working for various media organizations in the United Kingdom and the Netherlands; interviews with journalists working for teletext and viewdata systems in the UK and the Netherlands; questionnaires completed by journalists in the UK, the Netherlands, and Belgium; the author's observations of teletext and viewdata newsrooms in the UK and the Netherlands; analysis of the content of teletext systems in the UK as compared with the content of the BBC television news broadcasts and newspapers; and results of teletext audience studies in the UK and the Netherlands.

Interviews with Executives

Thanks to the help of Professor Jay G. Blumler, director of the Centre for Television Research at the University of Leeds in England, and Dr. Harold de Bock, Director of Audience Research for the Netherlands Broadcasting Foundation (NOS), I was able to interview the following executives from January through April of 1981: Hugh Whitcomb, Editorial Manager of Independent Television News Limited (providers of all news content to the Oracle teletext system) on January 19, 1981; Brian Botten, Managing Director of FINTEL (a subsidiary of *The Financial Times* and Extel, and one of the largest financial and business information providers to the Prestel viewdata system) on January 20, 1981; Geoffrey Hughes, Chief Executive of the Oracle teletext system, on January 20 and March 17, 1981; David Holmes, Chief Assistant to the Director General of the BBC, on January 21, 1981; Alan Protheroe, Deputy Director News and Current Affairs of the BBC, on January 21, 1981; Colin McIntyre, Editor of the Ceefax teletext service of the BBC, on February 3, 1981; Peter Hall, Editor of Oracle News, on February 4 and 5, 1981; Peter Wynne-Davies, Publicity, Prestel, on February 6, 1981; John Foxton, Marketing Manager of Viewtel (the Prestel viewdata electronic information service of the Birmingham *Post* and *Mail* Limited), on February 27, 1981; W. P. G. Stokla, Director of the Dutch Teletekst System, on March 11, 1981; Richard Hooper, Director of Prestel, March 16, 1981; and Alasdair McLeod, Manager of the Prestel Department, The Exchange Telegraph Company Limited (Extel) (the major provider of sports information to Prestel), on April 21, 1981.

Interviews with Researchers

In addition to these interviews, I also talked with several researchers studying videotex systems, including Peggy Gray of the Centre for Mass Communication Research at the University of Leicester in England, on February 26 and May 5, 1981; Dr. Harold de Bock, Director of Audience Research for the Netherlands Broadcasting Foundation (NOS), on March 12, 13 and 26, 1981; Pamela Mills and Michael Svennevig of the BBC Audience Research, on April 6, 1981; Werner and Blanca Degenhardt of the Institute for Communications Research, University of Munich, Germany, on May 11 and 12, 1981; and Frank Schumacher, Manager, Work Group for Communications Study, Munich, Germany, on May 11, 1981.

These interviews tended to concentrate on audience uses of and reactions to teletext systems (especially those with Peggy Gray, Harold de Bock, Pamela Mills and Michael Svennevig), and on the impact of videotex systems on existing media.

Interviews with Journalists and Observations of Newsrooms

I raised the questions listed earlier in this chapter with journalists working in the Independent Television News' Oracle newsroom on February 4 and 5, 1981; with journalists working in the BBC's Ceefax newsroom on February 12 and March 17, 1981; with those working in the Viewtel (Birmingham *Post* and *Mail*) newsroom on February 27, 1981; with journalists working in the Netherlands Broadcasting Foundation's "Teletekst" newsroom on March 11 and 12, 1981; and with those working in Oracle's London Weekend Television newsroom on March 17, 1981.

When I was in the offices, I tried to interview every journalist working and to raise as many of the questions on their work, the flow of news, and the impact of teletext and viewdata on other media as possible. Between interviews, I watched these journalists at work, paying special attention to news sources, news selection and updating decisions, interaction among journalists, and news writing techniques. Most of the journalists were very cooperative and open to my questions, even though they were constantly busy updating news stories. I took extensive notes during these interviews and dictated from these notes as soon as possible after each day's work.

Questionnaires Completed by Journalists

As mentioned earlier, I constructed a questionnaire for teletext and viewdata journalists that included measures of previous employment, job activities, perceptions of adequacy of news coverage, news sources, necessary job skills, professional attitudes, future intentions, perceptions of audiences, reporting methods, etc. (See Appendix 3 for this questionnaire.) After my personal interviews with and observations of these journalists, I asked them to complete the questionnaires and return them to me. Although the percentage of responses probably would have been higher if I had administered each questionnaire to each journalist, the demands of the job situation prevented this approach in most cases. It was not practical to interview most journalists after work because of their need to catch commuter trains.

Even with these constraints, I was able to obtain seven completed questionnaires from the nine journalists working for the Oracle teletext system,
nine completed questionnaires from the 20 journalists working for the
Ceefax teletext system, one completed questionnaire from the nine journalists working for the Netherlands Broadcasting Foundation teletext
system, and one completed questionnaire from the single journalist working
for the Belgian teletext system. From these 18 questionnaires, I feel confident in generalizing about the Oracle and Belgian teletext journalists, fairly
confident in generalizing about the Ceefax journalists, and not at all confident in generalizing about the Dutch teletext journalists. It must be
remembered, however, that my personal interviews with and observations
of all these journalists (except the one from Belgium) were used to supplement and corroborate the information from the questionnaires.

Comparative Content Analyses

Although this study is based primarily on interviews and observations, the
news content of the Oracle and Ceefax teletext systems for January 20,
1981, was compared with the content of the BBC's Channel 1 evening television news broadcast and with the news content of three national tabloid
newspapers (the *Daily Mail, The Sun,* and the *Daily Star*), the two leading
full-size national newspapers (*The Guardian* and *The Times*), and two provincial (regional) newspapers (the *Yorkshire Post* and the *Yorkshire Evening Post*) on the same date. This simple comparison was done for the purpose of comparing the number of news stories, and the number of words
devoted to each story, in each medium. It was not intended to be a
systematic, thorough content analysis of these media.

The news content of the Oracle and Ceefax systems was recorded with a
35 mm camera, the BBC1 news was recorded with an audio cassette
recorder and later transcribed, and the issues of the newspapers were purchased in Leeds, England, on January 30, 1981. This date was chosen
because it was a regular week day (Friday), because no particular story
seemed to dominate the news that day, and because it was a convenient time
for the photographing of Oracle and Ceefax teletext pages.

Another comparison of Oracle and Ceefax teletext news coverage with
newspaper news coverage was carried out on Sunday, April 12, 1981, the
day of the launching of the U.S. space shuttle Columbia and the day following the first rioting in Brixton, South London. In this case, the Oracle and
Ceefax news content was compared with *The Sunday Times* and the Mon-
day (April 13) coverage of *The Guardian* (not published on Sunday). This
date was chosen primarily to observe the constant updating capability of
teletext as applied to the continually unfolding story of the launching of the

space shuttle, and to see how the teletext systems would react to a day dominated by two major stories. As with the first comparison, the emphasis in this analysis was on the number of news stories devoted to each subject and the number of words within these stories, rather than on the qualititative aspects of the coverage.

Review of Audience Studies

In addition to the interviews, observations, and comparisons of content, the present study also draws upon the findings of two teletext audience surveys—one in the United Kingdom by Philips Electronics Video Division, and one in the Netherlands by the Netherlands Broadcasting Foundation (NOS) Audience Research Department. The "Superstats" on Prestel registrations and use, compiled by the British Post Office computers, are also employed for some of the conclusions regarding the viewdata audience in the United Kingdom.

The Philips Teletext Users Survey was conducted during 1979 and 1980 by the Consumer Market Research Department of Philips Video. It included only owners and renters of Philips color television sets equipped with a teletext decoder who were interested enough to agree to take part in the survey. To find persons with a Philips teletext set, a postage-paid coupon was included with each set sold, and Visionhire (a television rental firm) supplied information on those renting such sets. The data were collected from 609 persons in two stages: (1) A self-completed questionnaire designed to indicate who uses teletext and their opinions of the service; and (2) A diary completed by users to show the time and frequency of use, including details on which pages were viewed.[4]

The NOS teletext survey in the Netherlands was conducted in the fall of 1980 by the Audience Research Department of the Netherlands Broadcasting Foundation (NOS) under the direction of Dr. Harold de Bock. From about 2200 homes reported to have teletext receivers, 315 returned a card enclosed with each teletext receiver or responded to a request for volunteers on the teletext screen. From these 315 households, a sample of 227 persons 12 years and older was constructed. This sample was interviewed eight times during the fall of 1980 (October and November) concerning the frequency and times of viewing certain teletext pages, recall of teletext content, manner in which teletext pages are requested, reactions to the waiting time for teletext pages, appreciation of different kinds of teletext content (news, consumer items, weather and traffic information, sports, radio, and television information), desire for a hard copy printer, influence

---

[4]My thanks to Mr. Michael Imms of Philips Electronics Video Division for generously providing some details of this audience survey.

of teletext viewing on newspaper and magazine reading (and vice versa), and overall evaluation of teletext services.[5] The "Superstats" from the Prestel viewdata system provided information on the number of users of the system, the number of information providers to the system, the number of frames (pages) available from Prestel, the distribution of users by region of the country, the sales of viewdata TV sets and adaptors, and the kinds of business customers subscribing to Prestel.[6]

SUMMING UP

This chapter has described the methods used to gather information in England, the Netherlands, Germany, and Belgium on the effects of teletext and viewdata on journalists and their work, on the flow of news, and on newsroom organization and other media. It should be clear by now that a strategy of "multiple operationism," or the use of multiple methods, was used to gather this information. By relying not only on interviews, but also on observations, analysis of media content, and questionnaires, the study provides a more complete—and hopefully more accurate—picture of the overall situation.[7] In addition, the conclusions of this present study draw upon the many writings and studies reviewed in Chapter 2.

Although the economics and technology of teletext and viewdata systems are likely to be substantially different in countries other than those included in this study, such as the United States, many of the findings from this present study will apply to journalism, news, and communications media in these other countries because of the similarities in journalistic work, definitions of news, and characteristics of teletext and viewdata screen formats and capacities.

In the next three chapters I discuss these findings in detail, and Chapter 7 contains my conclusions and recommendations regarding the future development of videotex as a journalistic medium.

---

[5]Special thanks are due to my friend and colleague, Dr. Harold de Bock, Director of the Audience Research Department of the Netherlands Broadcasting Foundation, for taking the time to translate many of the questions and findings of this survey from Dutch to English.

[6]My thanks to Richard Hooper, Director of Prestel; John Foxton, Marketing Manager of Viewtel 202 of the Birmingham Post & Mail Ltd.; and Peter Wynne–Davies, Publicity, Prestel, for providing hard copies of these statistics for me.

[7]For an excellent discussion of the benefits of "multiple operationism," see Eugene Webb, Donald Campbell, Richard Schwartz, & Lee Sechrest, *Unobtrusive Measures: Nonreactive Research in the Social Sciences* (Chicago: Rand-McNally, 1966), especially pages 1–34.

4 Findings: Journalists and Their Work

This chapter presents findings on how teletext and viewdata presently affect journalists and their work. In reviewing these results, the reader should remember that they are based mainly on the state of videotex technology in Great Britain and the Netherlands in the first half of 1981. There is nothing fixed or absolute about them; as videotex technologies develop and change, so too may some of these conclusions. Yet perhaps these findings will stimulate some re-evaluations of teletext and viewdata as journalistic media before the patterns become established.

My interviews with teletext and viewdata journalists, observations of them at work, and their answers to my questionnaires revealed the following findings.

REPORTING

Journalists working for teletext systems in the United Kingdom and the Netherlands do almost no independent reporting. They rely primarily upon what others are writing in various wire services and newspapers.

Nearly all of the teletext journalists in Britain, the Netherlands, and Belgium spend 9 or 10 hours a day working in an office, and 6 to 9 hours of that time at a typewriter or computer terminal, with the majority spending 8 or 9 hours in this manner. Most spend one-half to 1 hour on the telephone, and none claim to spend any time outside the office reporting in Britain and Holland, but the chief editor of Belgian Radio and Television News, who runs the Belgian teletext system as part of his job, indicated that he spends 2 to 3 hours a day outside the office reporting.

These findings contrast with those of a recent study of about 400 randomly selected print and broadcast journalists in the United Kingdom by Philip Elliott of Leicester University. He found that 9% said their main job was information gathering, and two-thirds said they typically spent one-half their time or less in the office and 60% or *less* of their time at a typewriter or computer terminal.[1] Likewise, a study of 1313 randomly selected journalists in the United States in the early 1970s by John Johnstone and others found that 37.1% of the print journalists regularly covered a beat, as did 23.5% of the broadcast journalists.[2] Thus it appears that teletext journalists do far less out of the office reporting than do journalists who work for more conventional print and broadcast media. Teletext journalists are generally editors rather than reporters.

A number of factors contribute to this lack of outside reporting, including the need to constantly update teletext and viewdata news pages, the very limited space available for news (usually no more than 20 pages of 75 to 85 words each), the small size of the journalistic staffs (nine for the Oracle teletext system, 20 for the Ceefax teletext system, nine for the Dutch teletext system, one for Belgian teletext, and two for the Viewtel viewdata system), and the limited budgets for these systems, which are not likely to be substantially increased until they begin reaching larger audiences and generating revenues from advertising or other sources.

SKILLS

Writing concisely and designing pages on video display terminals (VDTs) are the primary skills required for a teletext or viewdata journalist, rather than reporting and information gathering. It is also necessary to be able to make news judgments quickly and to cope with a continuous deadline.

Because journalists working for teletext and viewdata systems are "information brokers" who select, package, and disseminate selected news stories rather than "information gatherers" who generate such stories from observations and interviews, it is not surprising that teletext journalists generally rate as very important writing and editing skills and "the ability to give a straightforward account of the facts of an incident." The UK journalists studied by Elliott also rate this ability as important (97% thought so), but these more conventional journalists rated "the ability to recognize 'the

---

[1] Personal communication and consultation with Philip Elliott, Centre for Mass Communication Research, University of Leicester, England, February 25 and 26, 1981, and May 5, 1981.

[2] John Johnstone, Edward Slawski, & William Bowman, *The News People* (Urbana: University of Illinois Press, 1976), p. 218.

story' in any assignment" and "the ability to give people a sense of personalities and atmosphere involved in an event" as considerably more important than did the teletext journalists from England and Belgium. The teletext journalists, on the other hand, rate "the ability to gather information from different sources quickly" as not particularly or only somewhat important.

In addition to learning to operate VDTs and to making decisions quickly about what to use and to discard, teletext and viewdata journalists must acquire some layout and design skills to be able to construct TV "pages" that are fairly attractive and readable, and that can stand alone from other pages. Such skills often involve the designing of headings for different sections or pages, the use of different colors to emphasize certain words or lines of type, and the use of spacing between paragraphs. Teletext and viewdata systems in Britain, the Netherlands, and Belgium also permit the use of still graphics (drawings, diagrams, etc.) formed from tiny squares of color on the screen. Although true curves are not possible with the English teletext and viewdata systems (they are with the Canadian Telidon system), nevertheless some very creative diagrams and drawings do appear on the English alpha-mosaic systems.

Because speed and updating are seen as the primary strengths of teletext and viewdata news, journalists working for these systems are similar to wire service editors or radio news editors who face "a constant rolling deadline" and many more stories than they can transmit during a day. During the 14 hours the Oracle teletext system was in operation on February 4, 1981, for example, there were 348 major changes made, or one major change (new story or update of old story) every 2½ minutes.

This vividly illustrates the continuous deadline in teletext and viewdata newsrooms. The space constraints on teletext and viewdata journalists are far greater than those for most other media, except perhaps radio. These constraints force videotex journalists to be extremely selective in their choice of news stories. They usually are limited to 20 or fewer general news stories (not counting sports, weather, traffic, television listings), most of which contain 75 to 85 words each. This is not as great a problem on a viewdata system such as Prestel where the number of pages is not as limited as on a teletext system, but even on Prestel most news stories don't run more than four or five pages in length because page access data indicate that the drop-off from the first page of such stories to the second is dramatic—75% or more for many stories.

In short, the skills required for teletext and viewdata journalism now are those related to rapid information processing and dissemination, not information collecting. This means that there is very little need for conventional reporting methods such as interviewing and unstructured observation, and even less need for advanced social science and other methods such as those used in interpretive, investigative, enterprise, "new journalism" or "precision journalism" reporting. Such advanced methods of gathering news information often are stressed in journalism schools in the United States today, as these schools seek to make journalists less dependent on other organizations and institutions for their pictures of society and the world.[3] But the present constraints of teletext and viewdata journalism offer almost no opportunity for the use of these reporting methods.

JOB SATISFACTION

Most journalists find working for teletext and viewdata very demanding, some find it boring, and many find it challenging and somewhat exciting to keep up with the very latest news. Overall, though, general levels of job satisfaction are not as high among teletext journalists as among U.S. print and broadcast journalists.

Because of the need for constant updating and extreme selectivity in choice of news stories and content from these stories, most of the journalists I interviewed found working for teletext and viewdata quite demanding, but many accepted the challenge of their work willingly and described it as stimulating. Some found the frequent monitoring of the wire service output and the corresponding updating of teletext content boring (one journalist referred to his teletext operation as "a word factory"), but his view seemed to be in the minority. The majority of the teletext journalists seemed to enjoy the challenge of the "constant rolling deadline" and the difficulty of condensing longer stories to a few short paragraphs for the TV screen.

But there are other aspects to working for teletext and viewdata operations that contribute to a generally lower level of satisfaction with work among teletext journalists than among journalists working for more traditional media. These include a lack of bylines on stories and thus a lack of personal recognition, a related lack of prestige as compared to working for better known media, little contact with other journalists on the job, less ability than many other journalists to indicate which stories are considered most important, and less chance to cover stories one thinks should be reported.

According to the teletext journalists I interviewed, many journalists working for more conventional media are openly scornful of those working for teletext and viewdata, calling them "hack rewriters" and referring to the Oracle system as "orifice," among other things. This lack of respect for videotex journalists on the part of other journalists is not helped by the rela-

---

[3]For more information on this point, see David Weaver & Maxwell McCombs, "Journalism and Social Science: A New Relationship?" *Public Opinion Quarterly*, 44: 477–494 (Winter 1981).

tive isolation of teletext and viewdata newsrooms. In both British teletext systems, the Dutch teletext operation, and the Birmingham *Post*'s Viewtel viewdata system (the primary news supplier to Prestel), the videotex newsrooms are widely separated from the other broadcast and newspaper newsrooms, making frequent communication between videotex and other journalists difficult. At times, journalists working in the other newsrooms will call or visit the videotex journalists with tips on breaking stories or suggested corrections, but these contacts are rare, occurring perhaps once or twice a day. Several of the teletext and viewdata journalists I interviewed remarked that they wished their newsrooms were "in a corner" of the regular newsrooms so they could interact more easily with the other journalists and have a better idea of what stories their colleagues were planning to emphasize in news broadcasts and the newspaper.

This separation of videotex journalists from others does not seem to be as prevalent in emerging systems in the United States as in Britain and the Netherlands. A survey of 28 operating electronic news delivery systems (including 14 cable news operations) in the States during the summer of 1981 by Linda Zaradich of Indiana University's School of Journalism revealed that 27% of the 22 systems with separate videotex staffs located these staffs in the same room with other journalists, and 45% of these systems had journalists located on the same floor as others. In addition, 55% of these systems reported regular contact between the videotex journalists and others. Ten of the 12 systems that reported this regular contact located their videotex journalists in the same room or on the same floor as other journalists.[4]

Another constraint on videotex journalists that may contribute to lower job satisfaction is their limited ability to indicate which news items they consider most important. Whereas many other journalists have some flexibility in placement and length of stories, teletext and viewdata journalists generally cannot vary the length of stories greatly and cannot use different sizes of type (or different amounts of film or tape) to indicate which stories they consider most important. Videotex journalists can vary the placement of a story in the overall list of stories, and can use different colors and flashing characters for emphasis. They can also make use of the "newsflash" page to emphasize what they consider to be the most recent and important story of the moment, but they are quite limited in story length and overall number of stories (especially on teletext systems.).

Because they depend so heavily on what others report, videotex journalists are also limited in their choice of stories to publish electronically. About one-fourth of the 18 teletext journalists who completed my question-

---

[4]Linda J. Zaradich, "Electronic News Delivery: A Survey of 35 Projects," School of Journalism and Center for New Communications, Indiana University, Bloomington, October 1981.

(Above) Newsroom of the BBC's Ceefax Teletext System in London.

(Below) Newsroom of the Independent Television Network's Oracle Teletext System in London.

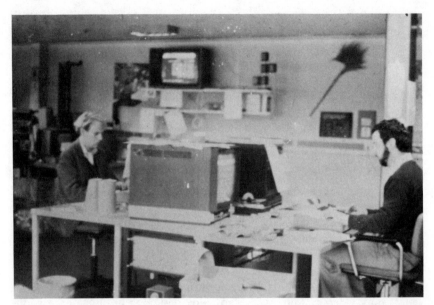

(Above) Newsroom of the Netherlands Broadcasting Foundation's Teletext System in Hilversum.

naire agreed that there were stories that should be covered but are not, whereas only about 6% of a national sample of some 400 United Kingdom journalists studied by Elliott felt that they could only occasionally follow up a good story idea. Among Elliott's journalists, 64% said that they could almost always follow up a good idea for a story, and 29% said they could more than not.

About one-sixth of the teletext journalists who completed my questionnaire also perceived their own news organizations as doing a "poor" job of informing the public, as compared to 2% of the 1313 U.S. journalists studied by Johnstone et al. in 1971. Even though about two-fifths of the teletext journalists rated their organizations' performance in informing the public as "very good" or "outstanding," 53% of the journalists studied by Johnstone et al. did so, suggesting that teletext journalists do not have quite as high an opinion of their news organizations as do other journalists working for more conventional media in the United States.

All of the factors just discussed seem to contribute to somewhat lower levels of job satisfaction among teletext journalists, as compared to those studied by Johnstone et al., and by Stephen Hess in Washington, D.C.[5] (See Table 4.1) Although only 1.2% of Johnstone's journalists and 2.1 of Hess' said they were "very dissatisfied" with their jobs, slightly more than one-tenth of the teletext journalists claimed to feel this way. However, Table 4.1

[5]Johnstone et al., *op. cit.,* p. 238; and Stephen Hess, *The Washington Reporters* (Washington, D.C.: The Brookings Institution, 1981), p. 141.

also reveals that the majority of teletext journalists felt "fairly" or "very" satisfied with their jobs, as did the journalists studied by Johnstone and Hess, suggesting that there are both rewards to working as a videotex journalist as well as frustrations and limitations.

One of the sources of satisfaction for teletext and viewdata journalists is the lack of anyone between them and the television screen. They generally write and edit their own stories without much, if any, supervision by an editor and without any interference by production workers, except perhaps at Oracle where keyboard operators type in the stories written by journalists. Although this lack of checking places a burden on videotex journalists to be especially careful regarding clarity, spelling, accuracy, libelous material, etc., it also gives many of them a sense of perceived autonomy and control over their work. All of the journalists at Ceefax and the Dutch Teletext operation I talked with preferred to type their own stories into the video display terminals, and not to work through keyboard operators. They argued that having journalists at the keyboards is faster than working through keyboard operators, allowing changes to be made more easily, and enabling journalists to control the appearance of the page as well as its content. Many videotex journalists also enjoy designing headings for various pages and having the freedom to experiment with different colors.

Although several journalists working for the Oracle system—where keyboard operators are employed—argued that these operators often serve as a check on accuracy, spelling, phrasing, etc., and can save journalists the drudgery of keyboarding routine material that does not require editorial judgment (share prices, sports scores, etc.), the majority of the journalists preferred to input their own material and construct their own pages. Some journalists working for the Oracle system even admitted waiting until the keyboard operators went home to input some feature material that was not as timely as news content. One journalist said she thought the keyboard operators were generally "bored to death."

SPECIALIZATION

Most teletext and viewdata journalists cannot specialize in a certain kind of news because of the smallness of staffs and the large volume of diverse news flowing into their offices. In addition, many of these journalists must deal with entertainment and advertising material as well as news.

Videotex journalists must be generalists. They must be able to process all kinds of information, especially if they work for teletext systems such as Oracle and Ceefax. A few are able to concentrate on sports or financial news, but they are in the minority, and often they and others are rotated between these areas and general news, depending on the needs and wishes of

TABLE 4.1
Job Satisfaction

Satisfaction Ratings	Johnstone's U.S. Journalists[a] (n = 1313)	Hess' Washington Reporters[b] (n = 192)	All Teletext Journalists[c] (n = 18)	Oracle Tele-text Journalists (n = 7)	Ceefax Teletext Journalists (n = 9)
Very satisfied	48.5%	40.1%	44.4%	42.9%	44.4%
Fairly satisfied	38.6	44.3	38.9	28.6	44.4
Somewhat dissatisfied	11.7	13.5	5.6	14.3	0.0
Very dissatisfied	1.2	2.1	11.1	14.3	11.1

[a]From a 1971 national survey of U.S. journalists reported in John Johnstone, Edward Slawski, & William Bowman, *The News People* (Urbana: University of Illinois Press, 1976), p. 238.

[b]From a 1978 survey of Washington, D.C. reporters described in Stephen Hess, *The Washington Reporters* (Washington, D.C.: The Brookings Institution, 1981), p. 141.

[c]The answers of the single Dutch and the single Belgian teletext journalists are included in these total percentages for all 18 teletext journalists, but are not reported individually to protect the confidentiality of responses. Although it is not generally sound practice to compute percentages with such small numbers, it is done here and in other tables for purposes of comparison with the other studies.

the organization. This lack of ability to specialize, coupled with the constant deadline pressures of their jobs, makes it difficult for teletext and viewdata journalists to critically evaluate much of the information they receive each day. They can, and do, compare accounts of the same events from different sources, and they do rate some sources as more dependable than others (Reuters news service is generally rated very high, especially for foreign news coverage, whereas United Press International is not), but in general these journalists pass along accounts of events they consider to be most important without much questioning of them. In rare instances, they may call one of the wire services for clarification or verification.

Because teletext, and especially viewdata, services provide information other than that traditionally defined as news, many journalists working for these systems must deal with entertainment material (puzzles, games, Valentine messages, film reviews, television and radio listings, theatre productions, holiday travel information, etc.) as well as news reports. As one journalist working for Independent Television's Oracle system in London put it, "You have to constantly strike a balance between entertainment and information to satisfy the various television companies throughout the country." Colin McIntyre, editor of the BBC's Ceefax teletext service, argues that teletext is a form of broadcasting and therefore should entertain as well as inform because people are used to viewing television mainly for entertainment. As he puts it, in answer to the question of whether teletext should be considered an entertainment as well as information medium:

> The answer is—unequivocally—yes!
>
> The BBC is in show business. Except for a few early years under Lord Reith, when it broadcast what it thought the public *ought* to want, it always has been in show business, truly responsive to what the public wants.[6]

McIntyre adds that, "Whatever they say when questioned by sociologists and market researchers, what people expect from television is *entertainment*."[7] He claims that those at Ceefax have learned a lesson from "surveys which placed the 'fun and games' pages of BBC 2 only a little behind news, weather, and program guides in popularity. We now have puzzles, quizzes, and competitions; word-games and chess problems; hobby corners and features about gardening, cooking, and dressmaking. All entertainment."[8] McIntyre concludes that broadcasting, "is not concerned with only the serious matters of life."[9]

In addition to handling material that might be classified more as enter-

---

[6]Colin McIntyre, "CEEFAX—an editorial update," *European Broadcasting Union Review,* 32 (March 1981), p. 49.
[7]*Ibid.*
[8]*Ibid.*
[9]*Ibid.*

tainment than news, journalists working for commercial teletext and view-data systems are beginning to have to be concerned about the content of advertising messages, especially those ads that run at the bottom of news or entertainment. As one teletext executive put it, "The editor would not want to have a news story about a Pan American air crash on the same page as a commercial for Pan American airlines."

It seems likely that in a commercial teletext or viewdata operation, jour-nalists would be responsible for placing advertising messages on a page as well as news and entertainment content, in contrast to the sharp division of advertising and editorial functions in most conventional commercially bas-ed media. If so, this could pose real problems in situations where jour-nalistic and commercial values conflict. For example, many journalists would probably find it ethically repugnant to write advertising messages for organizations which are being investigated for wrongdoing by other jour-nalists. In fact, many journalists probably would find it ethically ques-tionable to write advertising messages for any commercial firm, whether under investigation or not. However, one executive associated with the Oracle teletext system said that they "would have to learn to live with com-mercials." None of the teletext or viewdata journalists I interviewed ex-pressed serious reservations about writing advertising messages. The only concerns expressed by some journalists working for Oracle were that the advertising messages would further reduce the number of words possible on a page.

BACKGROUNDS

Journalists working for teletext and viewdata systems in Britain and the Netherlands come mainly from *print* media backgrounds rather than from broadcast. And most come from newspapers, rather than wire services or specialist publications.

Slightly more than 60% of the teletext journalists in Britain who completed my questionnaire had worked as newspaper reporters. Nearly 40% had been newspaper editors of some kind, and about one-fifth had worked for a magazine or specialist publication, or for radio. (See Table 4.2) This preponderance of print media experience is not surprising, when one con-siders that teletext and viewdata are both primarily word-oriented, rather than orally or visually oriented, media. As one executive said, "I look for the tightest rewrite sub-editors I can find." Another editor remarked that he looks for "good, tight, hard subs who can take out all the flannel and get it down to the basics" because "every word has to count."

One Oracle executive remarked that initially some editors from broadcast media were hired as teletext journalists, but now most of the staff comes from print media because "print journalists are more used to writing con-

TABLE 4.2
Previous Job Experience

Past Employment (multiple answers permitted)	Elliott's UK Journalists[a] (n = 151)	All Teletext Journalists[b] (n = 18)	Oracle Journalists (n = 7)	Ceefax Journalists (n = 9)
Newspaper reporter	55.1%	61.1%	100.0%	44.4%
Newspaper editor	39.1	38.9	14.3	55.6
Editorial writer	24.5	5.6	0.0	11.1
Wire service or news agency	0.0	16.7	42.9	0.0
Department chief	44.4	0.0	0.0	0.0
Magazine or special- list publication	0.0	22.2	14.3	22.2
Radio	6.6	22.2	28.6	11.1
Television	6.6	16.7	14.3	11.1
Photography	10.6	0.0	0.0	0.0
Other jobs	43.0	33.3	14.3	44.4

[a]From a 1980–81 survey of about 400 randomly selected journalists in the United Kingdom conducted by Philip Elliott of the Centre for Mass Communication Research at the University of Leicester, England. Report not yet published.

[b]These total percentages are based on the answers of the single Dutch and the single Belgian teletext journalists, as well as the Oracle and Ceefax journalists. The Dutch journalist had worked as a newspaper editor and as a magazine journalist, as well as in other jobs. The Belgian journalist had worked for both radio and television.

cisely than are broadcast journalists." He added that those who write for television news need to be sensitive to the complementary relationship between news content and pictures, whereas those who write for print media generally try to tell the entire story in words alone. Another viewdata executive said that he tried to hire journalists who were content with being "deskbound," and who were not "too set in their ways." He argued that the younger journalists were usually more flexible than the older, and some of them regarded working with video display terminals (VDTs) as good experience for the future technology likely to be used in Fleet Street national newspapers and in other publications. This executive said that none of his viewdata journalists come from Fleet Street newspapers or from television stations, largely because these organizations pay higher salaries than his organization does, although his pays more than the provincial (regional and local) newspapers in Britain and about the same as the news agencies and London magazines.

According to one teletext editor, even if a journalist is able to write concisely and to condense longer stories to fit the constraints of a teletext or viewdata page, it takes 2 or 3 months to train that person to be fully competent with the equipment and the procedures in a teletext or viewdata newsroom. This sub-editor claimed that, "It's murder to introduce a new person and still get everything else done." And she obviously favored a highly stable staff, but teletext journalists' answers to my questionnaires suggest that her wish may be less realistic than if she were working for more conventional media in the United States.

As Table 4.3 shows, only about one-third of all teletext journalists expect to be working for the same organization in five years, whereas nearly twice that proportion expect to be, among the U.S. journalists studied by Johnstone. Among the teletext journalists, it is clear that substantially more of those employed by the Oracle system expect to be working for the same organization in five years than do those working for Ceefax.

ROLES AND ETHICS

Whereas the opinions of teletext journalists on the acceptability of various reporting methods generally parallel those of other journalists, teletext journalists' views on their roles and the functions of their media organizations generally differ from the views of other journalists.

TABLE 4.3
Employment Aspirations

Five Years From Now Expect to be:	Johnstone's U.S. Journalists[a] (n = 1313)	All Teletext Journalists[b] (n = 18)	Oracle Journalists (n = 7)	Ceefax Journalists (n = 9)
Working for same organization	62.0%	33.3%	57.1%	11.1%
Working elsewhere in news media	21.8	33.3	14.3	44.4
Working outside news media	6.6	16.7	14.3	22.2
Retired	1.4	5.6	0.0	11.1
Undecided	8.2	11.1	14.3	11.1

[a]From a 1971 national survey of U.S. journalists reported in John Johnstone, Edward Slawski, and William Bowman, *The News People* (Urbana: University of Illinois Press, 1976), p. 239.

[b]These total percentages are based on the answers of the single Dutch and the single Belgian teletext journalists, as well as the Oracle and Ceefax journalists. The Dutch and Belgian answers are not reported individually to protect the confidentiality of responses.

Despite the fact that the teletext journalists I studied do almost no independent reporting, nearly two-thirds of them have worked in the past as newspaper reporters, as indicated in Table 4.2, so it is not surprising that their opinions on the acceptability of various reporting methods are generally similar to the opinions of the UK journalists studied by Elliott. As Table 4.4 shows, more than two-thirds of Elliott's journalists agreed that four of the reporting practices might be justified: paying people involved in stories for information, using confidential business or government documents without authorization, badgering unwilling informants to get a story, and getting employed in an organization to gain inside information. One-half or more of the teletext journalists agreed with the first three of these practices (they were not asked about the fourth). The reporting practice least likely to be approved by both conventional and teletext journalists was agreeing to protect confidentiality and not doing so.

About one-third of both groups of journalists thought that claiming to be somebody else might be justified, and about one-half agreed with making use of personal documents without permission—substantially fewer than agreed to using government or business documents. The practice most likely to be approved by teletext journalists was quoting an unnamed source rather than giving the person's name (not asked of the other journalists). Nearly two-thirds of the teletext journalists also approved of using hidden cameras and hidden microphones for important stories; the others were not asked about these practices. Among the teletext journalists, however, it is apparent that the Ceefax journalists were less likely (sometimes dramatically so) to approve of these various reporting methods than were the Oracle journalists, except for running stories quoting unnamed sources. This practice was approved by more than four-fifths of each group. (See Table 4.4)

Thus, while the reporting ethics of both teletext and more conventional journalists appear to be fairly similar, there are rather sharp differences between the Oracle and Ceefax journalists. This may be because of the non-commercial nature of the British Broadcasting Corporation and the differences in previous job experiences of the two groups of journalists (Ceefax journalists were substantially more likely to have been newspaper editors than were the Oracle group, and the Oracle journalists were twice as likely to have been reporters). Perhaps working as a reporter hardens one to the "realities" of prying information from unwilling sources and the necessity of using questionable methods to obtain such information.

Although there are only minor differences between teletext and other journalists' views on reporting practices, there are more noticeable differences in the importance assigned to various aspects of their jobs. Table 4.5 shows that teletext journalists assign less importance to public service and to job security than do the U.S. journalists studied by Johnstone et al. in 1971, but more importance to pay. Both teletext and other journalists

TABLE 4.4
Reporting Methods

Percent Agreeing That the Following Might be Justified:	Elliott's UK Journalists[a] (n = 356)	All Teletext Journalists[b] (n = 18)	Oracle Journalists (n = 7)	Ceefax Journalists (n = 9)
Using confidential business or government documents	86.0%	66.7%	100.0%	55.6%
Getting employed to gain inside information	73.3	—[c]	—	—
Badgering unwilling informants	71.9	72.2	71.4	66.7
Paying people for information	68.5	50.0	71.4	44.4
Using personal documents without permission	52.0	44.4	71.4	33.3
Claiming to be somebody else	32.6	33.3	42.9	33.3
Agreeing to protect confidentiality and not doing so	3.7	5.6	14.3	0.0
Using unnamed sources	—[c]	83.3	85.7	88.9
Using hidden cameras	—	61.1	85.7	55.6
Using hidden microphones	—	61.1	85.7	55.6

[a]From a 1980–81 survey of about 400 randomly selected journalists in the United Kingdom conducted by Philip Elliott of the Centre for Mass Communication Research at the University of Leicester, England. Report not yet published.
[b]These total percentages are based on the answers of the single Dutch and the single Belgian teletext journalists, as well as the Oracle and Ceefax journalists. The Dutch and Belgian answers are not reported individually to protect the confidentiality of their responses.
[c]Not asked of these journalists.

rated autonomy and freedom from supervision as quite important, especially those employed by the BBC's Ceefax operation.

Considering that only half as many teletext journalists expect to be working for the same organization in five years as do U.S. journalists (see Table 4.3) it is not surprising that teletext journalists rate job security as less important than Americans do. Considering the limitations of teletext as a journalistic medium, it is not unexpected that teletext journalists consider public service (the chance to help people) as less important than do the U.S. journalists working for conventional print and broadcast media. The fact that teletext journalists rated pay as more important than do the U.S. journalists studied by Johnstone et al. in 1971 may be the result of the relatively higher pay for teletext jobs as well as the severe constraints on the ability of these journalists to gather and report news.

The importance of various functions performed by news organizations was also evaluated differently by teletext journalists than by those working for more traditional media. Not surprisingly, teletext journalists thought that it was less important than did the U.S. journalists for their news organizations to investigate claims and statements made by the government, provide analysis and interpretation of complex problems, discuss national policy while it is still being developed, and cultivate intellectual and cultural interests of the public. (See Table 4.6) On the other hand, the teletext journalists rated getting information to the public quickly as more important than did the others. All journalists agreed that staying away from stories where factual content cannot be verified, and concentrating on news which is of interest to the widest possible public, are important news media functions.

These findings underscore the lack of original reporting by teletext journalists and the constraints imposed by the limited number of pages, and the limited word capacity, of teletext pages. Because one of the primary strengths of teletext is speed, it follows that getting information to the public as quickly as possible should be rated as extremely important by teletext journalists, especially by the Oracle journalists who do not deal with less timely feature material.

In evaluating other media functions not listed in Table 4.6 and not asked of Johnstone's journalists, Ceefax journalists rated as more important than did Oracle journalists the providing of entertainment and relaxation, advising and helping people, and being a proponent of new ideas. The Oracle journalists thought that it was more important to be a mirror of life than did the Ceefax staff. Again, the differences between the noncommercial BBC Ceefax operation (with its emphasis on other content besides news) and the commercial, news-oriented Oracle system partially explain these findings, but do not fully account for them. In the case of teletext and other media, it is unlikely that economic structures and organizational patterns can ever fully predict differences in journalistic values and attitudes.

PERCEPTIONS OF AUDIENCES, OTHER JOURNALISTS

Teletext journalists are more confident than others that journalists generally know what their viewers want, and that there are not great differences between the opinions

TABLE 4.5
Importance of Job Aspects
(Average Scores)

Job Aspect	Johnstone's U.S. Journalists[1]		All Teletext Journalists[2] (n = 18)	Oracle Journalists (n = 7)	Ceefax Journalists (n = 9)
	Print (n = 1030)	Broadcast (n = 283)			
Public service—the chance to help people	1.57[a]	1.66	1.00	0.86	1.11
Autonomy	1.48	1.48	1.45	1.29	1.67
Freedom from supervision	1.40	1.35	1.33	1.43	1.33
Job security	1.34	1.34	0.89	1.14	0.89
Pay	1.04	1.18	1.39	1.57	1.56
Fringe Benefits	0.98	0.92	0.61	0.71	0.67
Chance to get ahead	—[b]	—	0.94	1.14	1.00
Editorial policies	—	—	1.06	1.00	1.11

0 = not too important
1 = fairly important
2 = very important

[a]Not asked of these journalists.
[1]From a 1971 national survey of U.S. journalists reported in John Johnstone, Edward Slawski, and William Bowman, *The News People* (Urbana: University of Illinois Press, 1976), p. 229.
[2]These total scores are based on the answers of the single Dutch and the single Belgian teletext journalists, as well as the Oracle and Ceefax journalists. The Dutch and Belgian answers are not reported individually to protect the confidentiality of their responses.

of viewers and of journalists. Teletext journalists are also less likely to believe that there are great differences in political attitudes among journalists.

Although many teletext journalists, especially at the Oracle system, complained of a lack of audience reaction to their work, they were less likely than other UK journalists to agree that journalists often have wrong ideas about what the public wants or that great differences exist between the opinions of journalists and their audience members. (See Table 4.7.)

TABLE 4.6
Importance of Media Functions
(Average Scores)

Media Function	Johnstone's U.S. Journalists[1] (n = 1313)	All Teletext Journalists[2] (n = 18)	Oracle Journalists (n = 7)	Ceefax Journalists (n = 9)
Investigative claims of government	2.71[a]	1.44	1.57	1.33
Provide analysis of complex problems	2.45	1.72	1.42	1.78
Get information to public quickly	2.40	2.84	3.00	2.67
Discuss national policy	2.34	1.39	1.29	1.11
Stay away from stories where facts can't be verified	2.15	2.28	2.00	2.89
Concentrate on news of widest interest	2.02	2.22	2.29	2.22
Develop intellectual and cultural interests of the public	1.88	0.99	0.57	1.11
Provide entertainment and relaxation	1.48	1.39	1.00	2.00

[a]0 = not really important at all
 1 = somewhat important
 2 = quite important
 3 = extremely important

[1]From a 1971 national survey of U.S. journalists reported in John Johnstone, Edward Slawski, and William Bowman, *The News People* (Urbana: University of Illinois Press, 1976), p. 230.

[2]These total scores are based on the answers of the single Dutch and the single Belgian teletext journalists, as well as the Oracle and Ceefax journalists. The Dutch and Belgian answers are not reported individually to protect the confidentiality of their responses.

The Oracle journalists were nearly twice as likely as those working for Ceefax to agree that journalists generally know what their readers or viewers want, and much less likely than those at Ceefax to believe that journalists often have completely wrong ideas about what the public wants. This questionable sense of confidence among the Oracle staff is both ironic and understandable, given the lack of feedback from audiences to the ITN Oracle newsroom. The Ceefax journalists, who seemed to receive considerably more audience feedback, developed a more realistic view of the relationship (or lack of it) between journalistic and public priorities, a view closer to that held by British journalists in general, according to Table 4.7.

Both Oracle and Ceefax journalists were considerably less likely than UK journalists studied by Elliott to think that there are especially great differences in political attitudes among journalists. Although more than four-fifths of the UK journalists studied by Elliott thought so, less than one-half of the teletext journalists did. This difference probably reflects the youth and relative inexperience of teletext journalists, as well as their isolation from other journalists.

These findings suggest that teletext journalists need the reactions of audiences and other journalists to maintain a realistic perspective about their views and their work. Such reactions also seem to contribute to higher levels of satisfaction with one's job, especially at Ceefax and at the Birmingham *Post* and *Mail's* Viewtel system. The journalists I talked with at the Viewtel system stressed the importance of being able to get immediate feedback from the Prestel computer on the number of people reading each of their pages. Teletext journalists cannot obtain such rapid and precise estimates of the numbers of viewers for each page, but must rely on audience surveys for rougher estimates. But both teletext and viewdata journalists, like those working for more conventional media, must rely on letters, calls, and audience research for people's evaluations of their work. As the Viewtel journalists argued, however, this would not have to be the case with viewdata systems such as Prestel, where viewers could be asked to rate various kinds of content with multiple choice scales displayed on viewdata pages. These responses could be tabulated by the Prestel computer, just as the number of page accesses currently are. In this manner, polls and readership surveys could be done with the viewdata system itself rather than by telephone or in person. Of course, such a procedure would rely on self-selected samples, rather than more representative random samples, and this could pose a serious problem for generalizing the results to all viewers unless the response rates among all viewers were very high.

Overall, the findings that teletext journalists are more confident than others that journalists know what their readers want, and that there are not great differences between the opinions of readers and journalists, are troubling, because they suggest that the content of teletext systems is not

TABLE 4.7
Journalists and Their Audiences

Percent Agreeing That:	Elliott's UK Journalists[a] (n = 356)	All Teletext Journalists[b] (n = 18)	Oracle Journalists (n = 7)	Ceefax Journalists (n = 9)
Journalists generally know what audiences want	61.2%	61.1%	85.7%	44.4%
Journalists often have wrong ideas about what public wants	53.9	38.9	14.3	55.6
It is very important for a journalist to be in touch with public opinion	94.4	88.9	100.0	88.9
It is not of great importance for a journalist to know what people think of an issue	9.6	11.1	0.0	0.0
There is a great difference between the opinions of readers/viewers and of journalists	40.0	27.8	14.3	33.3
Journalists and the public generally have quite similar views on most issues	41.0	44.5	14.3	55.6
Among journalists, there are great differences in political attitudes	82.6	44.4	57.1	33.3
Most journalists think very much alike on political matters	8.4	16.7	14.3	22.2

[a]From a 1980–81 survey of about 400 randomly selected journalists in the United Kingdom conducted by Philip Elliott of the Centre for Mass Communication Research at the University of Leicester, England. Report not yet published.

[b]These total percentages are based on the answers of the single Dutch and the single Belgian teletext journalists, as well as the Oracle and Ceefax journalists. The Dutch and Belgian answers are not reported individually to protect the confidentiality of their responses.

likely to be experimented with or changed much unless there are loud and frequent protests from viewers. There have been very few audience surveys of teletext and viewdata users to date; and they have been given relatively little attention by the journalists I interviewed, perhaps because they are seldom seen by working journalists.

PERCEPTIONS OF IMPACT

Most teletext journalists view electronic news delivery technology as either benefitting editors and reporters, readers, and advertisers, or having little effect on them. Most predict that this technology will make no difference to newspaper proprietors and management, but a few predict harmful effects. And most predict harmful effects for compositors, typists, and other print workers.

Many teletext journalists become quite interested in videotex technology and "get hooked on it," but they are rather divided in their opinions regarding the benefits of this new technology for journalists and the public. Slightly more than one-half the teletext journalists answering my questionnaire thought that editors stood to benefit from the introduction of electronic news delivery technology, whereas nearly 40% thought that reporters would benefit. Most of the others thought that the technology would make no difference to editors and reporters. Ceefax journalists were considerably more likely than those working for Oracle to think that videotex technology would benefit reporters, newspaper owners and managers, and advertisers, thus reflecting more overall optimism about teletext than the other group.

About two-thirds of all teletext journalists thought that the technology would benefit readers, with the other third about evenly split between thinking it would make no difference to them or harm them. The journalists were about equally split on whether this new technology would harm advertisers or make no difference to them, with a few predicting harmful effects for advertising breaks between television programs because of viewers being able to switch to teletext material to avoid the TV ads.

Most teletext journalists agreed that the technology would harm compositors, typists, and other print workers, but a few thought that it would make no difference to them because their skills would be needed for teletext and viewdata systems. A few thought that "devotees of longer, more wordy news stories" would be harmed by videotex, and several cited television set manufacturers and various minorities as benefitting from it.

Nearly two-thirds of the teletext journalists completing the questionnaire thought that electronic news delivery technology would make no difference to newspaper proprietors and managers, with the majority of the remaining third predicting harmful effects.

It is not too surprising that there is most agreement among teletext journalists with respect to the effects of videotex on editors and readers, because they are most familiar with the actual impact of the technology on their own jobs and on the material they present to readers. But the impact of videotex technology on reporters, newspaper owners and managers, and advertisers in England and Holland (and other countries) has been negligible thus far, as we shall see in the next chapter, so opinions about effects on these groups are necessarily more speculative in nature.

These findings with regard to videotex journalists and their work in England, Holland, and Belgium suggest that there are not many opportunities for independent reporting on either teletext or viewdata systems, nor are there many chances for specialization in content area. This seems to be the emerging pattern in the United States as well. In the survey of 28 operating and seven planned videotex and cable news systems in the U.S. mentioned earlier, Linda Zaradich found in the four broadcast teletext systems that about 60% of the news came from the wire services, with another 16% from various news services, 20% from a newspaper staff, and only 3% from the teletext journalists themselves.[10] In the three U.S. viewdata systems, *none* of the news material was reported to come from the viewdata journalists themselves, but nearly 60% came from various newspaper staffs, with the remainder coming from wire and news services. This pattern also held for the 14 cable news systems studied by Zaradich, and generally for the seven CompuServe information providers (Associated Press member newspapers tied into a national telephone-based viewdata system), although about 10% of the news on this system was reported to come from the four employees hired specifically for electronic news delivery.

In addition to not being able to do much, if any, reporting, it is clear that videotex journalists tend to be young, relatively inexperienced, drawn primarily from print media backgrounds, and to have views on the roles of their news organizations that are focused more on information dissemination than on investigation and analysis. Perhaps because of their youth and relative isolation from other journalists, British and Dutch teletext journalists are more confident than others that they know what viewers want and that there are not great differences in political attitudes among journalists in general.

But, as mentioned earlier, this lack of regular contact with other journalists does not seem to be as pronounced in developing U.S. electronic delivery systems. Zaradich found in her survey that nearly one-third of the electronic journalists worked in the same room with other journalists, and

---

[10]Zaradich, *op. cit.*, p. 6.

nearly one half worked on the same floor. More than one-half reported that they were "in regular contact" with other journalists.[11]

In view of the limits on journalists and their work imposed by teletext and viewdata systems, and the generally lower levels of job satisfaction, it is surprising to find that most of these journalists view videotex technology as either benefitting journalists or having no effect on them. This suggests that many videotex journalists have not had the opportunity to do much reporting or that they are not much interested in doing such reporting, especially not in-depth or investigative reporting. It would be interesting to get the reactions of more seasoned reporters to working under the constraints of teletext and viewdata systems. The scorn for these systems by some other journalists, reported by the teletext journalists I interviewed, suggests that some of the more experienced print and broadcast reporters would not find much fulfillment in working for these systems unless they, like some now working for them, became "hooked" on the technology.

In the next chapter I deal with the effects of teletext and viewdata (or lack of them) on the flow of news and information, and try to shed additional light on the levels of job satisfaction and status just discussed.

---

[11] *Ibid.*

5 Findings: The Flow of News and Information

The interviews, observations, and comparisons of content suggest the following findings with regard to the impact of teletext and viewdata on the present flow of information.

INFORMATION DISTRIBUTION

At present, teletext and viewdata systems are mainly information *distribution* rather than information *gathering* devices. They generally do not provide "new" information not available from other media.

Although both teletext and viewdata systems presently carry little information that can't be found in other media, they do provide the "power of recall" that hasn't been possible before with broadcast information, except through the use of audio and video recorders which are not terribly convenient methods for retrieving specific items of news or information. Most of the news carried by teletext and viewdata systems in England and the Netherlands originates with the wire services or news agencies. News can be updated more quickly on teletext and viewdata systems than on other public media, but it does not differ much from the news of other media, except that it tends to be shorter and less detailed. Some information, such as seat availability on airline flights, updated train schedules, updated prices, and updated radio and television schedules, is not readily available through other public media, except perhaps the telephone, but this kind of information tends to be a small fraction of the present content of teletext systems.

It is fairly clear, too, that teletext and viewdata systems tend to reinforce the news agenda set largely by the wire services and the newspapers. Not only does most of the news content of teletext and viewdata systems in Britain and the Netherlands come from the wire services, but Ceefax regularly monitors Oracle, Oracle does the same with Ceefax, Viewtel (the main news provider to Prestel) uses Oracle at times to update its financial news, Oracle uses Prestel at times to update its American Express financial information and travel news, and the Dutch teletext systems checks the Krantel viewdata system in the Netherlands at times for news. In addition, teletext journalists in both England and Holland regularly scan newspapers, listen to radio news, and watch television news to keep up with the latest happenings, but they do almost no original reporting.[1] This does not mean that the teletext and viewdata systems all carry the same news stories, but it does mean that they tend to select their news from the larger pool provided by the major newspapers, wire services, and television news operations. Without their own reporters, they have little other choice, except to subscribe to more specialized publications and news services.

At present, then, teletext and viewdata are not contributing much to increasing the *diversity* of news, but they are making some of the latest news immediately and conveniently available to nearly half a million persons in the United Kingdom and nearly a quarter million in the Netherlands, assuming about three persons for each teletext or viewdata TV set. Some persons, such as the director of the Dutch Teletekst, W. P. G. Stokla, argue that there is no need for *more* news, but there is a need for *more available* news, a need that teletext serves well in his opinion. Others, such as the director of the Prestel viewdata system, Richard Hooper, argue that unique information and services are the key to the widespread adoption of viewdata systems.

NEW MEDIA

Teletext and viewdata are not strikingly "new media" in the sense of providing stimuli (such as sound, moving pictures, etc.) that the more established media don't already furnish. And teletext and viewdata are not "electronic newspapers" because they contain only a small portion of the content of a newspaper, most of it not local in nature.

---

[1]This lack of reporting is dramatically illustrated by the answers to the questionnaire item on how many hours in an average day teletext journalists spent outside the office reporting. All of the journalists responding from the Oracle, Ceefax, and Dutch Teletekst systems reported *zero* hours. The Belgian teletext journalist reported 1–2 hours a day outside the office reporting. Average number of hours per day spent on the telephone for Oracle journalists was one-half (30 minutes), slightly higher for Ceefax journalists, and one for both Dutch and Belgian teletext journalists. In contrast, the average number of hours per day spent at a typewriter or computer terminal was nine for Oracle journalists, nearly eight for those from Ceefax, and six for the Dutch teletext journalists. The Belgian teletext journalist did not report a figure for this activity.

Although videotext systems in general have been called "electronic newspapers," in their present form they lack much of the content normally associated with quality newspapers, including photographs, local classified and display advertising, in-depth news stories and columns, and a wide variety of local, national, and international news. Teletext systems at present usually offer 20 or fewer pages (TV screenfuls) of general news stories (excluding financial, sports, weather, travel, and television information). Each page contains a maximum of 24 lines of 40 characters each, which in practice translates into four or five paragraphs of three or four lines each, or about 75 to 80 words a page. It has been estimated that it would take about 70 teletext pages to contain the same number of words on one full page of a quality newspaper, so at present the British teletext systems are providing somewhere between one-fourth and one-third of a newspaper page of general news at any given time.

Because of the limited number of pages and the extremely short news stories (most don't exceed one screenful in length), teletext systems are more similar to radio news bulletins than newspapers. In fact, several persons I interviewed referred to teletext as "printed radio." Viewdata, on the other hand, was compared more often to an electronic bookstore or an electronic magazine because of the great number of pages (approaching 200,000 on the Prestel system) of very diverse information, much of it commercial in nature. However, even with nearly unlimited page capacity, viewdata systems such as Prestel rarely carry longer, more complex articles, columns, editorials, etc. The data on page use compiled by the Prestel computers shows that the drop-off in readership from the first page of a news story to the second is dramatic (up to 75% or 80%), suggesting that long, complex articles aren't well-suited to viewdata, and certainly not to teletext where the waiting time for the next page may be 20 to 30 seconds. This finding is consistent with other studies discussed in Chapter 2. With improvements in screen resolution and word capacity, and changes in reading habits, longer articles might be more acceptable on teletext or viewdata in the future, but at present such articles don't seem to work well on the television screen.[2]

---

[2]The only evidence to contradict this conclusion comes from the Viewtron viewdata system tested by Knight-Ridder Newspapers in Coral Gables, Florida. Two persons closely associated with the system and the research on it told this writer that news stories of 12 to 15 pages (TV screens) in length were read by "enough" viewers. And Philip Meyer, formerly Director of News Research for Knight-Ridder Newspapers and now Kenan Professor of Journalism at the University of North Carolina, wrote in a recent paper presented to the VIDEOTEX '81 conference in Toronto that "contrary to the reported Prestel experience, they (users of Viewtron) had the patience to read long stories, dutifully pushing the button to turn the pages a dozen times or more." See *VIDEOTEX '81: International Conference & Exhibition* (Middlesex, United Kingdom: Online Conferences, 1981), pp. 235–36. Meyer did caution, however, "It is too soon to tell whether the economics of publishing electronically will permit intense focusing on the local community." (p. 236).

(Above and Below) News Story with Illustration from the BBC's Ceefax Teletext System.

(Above) News Story from the ITV's Oracle Teletext System.

Even with additional pages being immediately available on viewdata systems, and available with no effort by the viewer on constantly cycling teletext "extended pages," reading long articles on the TV screen is a bit similar "to reading *War and Peace* on flash cards."[3]

In contrast to most newspapers in the United States and most newspapers outside London in England, nearly all news content of Ceefax, Oracle, and Prestel is national or international in scope (not local or even regional) although there are plans to begin providing regional teletext pages fairly soon.[4] This is due to the lack of reporting staff and the reliance on wire ser-

[3]See Douglas Watts (Staff Counsel for the American Newspaper Publishers Association), "Problems for Newspapers Introducing Electronic Transmission," in John W. Ahlhauser, ed., *Electronic Home News Delivery: Journalistic and Public Policy Implications* (Bloomington, Indiana: School of Journalism and Center for New Communications, 1981), p. 5.

[4]Personal interview with Hugh Whitcomb, Editorial Manager, Independent Television News Limited, London, January 19, 1981, and Geoffrey Hughes, Chief Executive, Oracle, London, January 20, 1981. See also "Scots Consult Their Own Oracle," *Broadcast,* 20 July 1981, p. 7, for a prediction that Scottish television would be launching Britain's "first regional teletext service" in Autumn 1981.

vices, the lack of sizable local audiences, and the lack of local advertising support. It would seem that local advertisers (both classified and retail) will not be as greatly interested in teletext and viewdata until a high percentage of homes in their geographic areas receive these systems. Without such advertising support, however, it is difficult to bring down the price of teletext—and especially viewdata—receivers to the point where they will appeal to a mass audience, and it is costly to employ local reporters. In a non-commercial operation such as the BBC, which is funded primarily from the license fees paid on each television set, it is difficult to justify sharply increased expenditures for local news coverage when such coverage does not increase the revenues of the organization. An additional fee for teletext TV sets has been considered, but does not seem feasible now when the emphasis is on reducing the price of teletext and viewdata receivers. As pointed out in Chapter 2, other studies indicate that expenditures for teletext and viewdata services by the general public for home use have been very modest so far, and are likely to remain that way unless services other than news delivery (shopping, banking, mail delivery, education, group participation, etc.) make such systems appear much more attractive than they do today.

TELETEXT VERSUS VIEWDATA

At present, teletext seems superior to viewdata for distributing news to the general public because of ease of use, relatively low cost, and ability to serve millions of users simultaneously.

It seems likely that teletext systems such as Ceefax and Oracle will continue to be more suited to the delivery of news to mass audiences than will viewdata systems for the foreseeable future. Various factors suggest a mass market for teletext and a largely commercial or elite market for viewdata in the near future. These factors include cost, ease of use, unlimited audience size, and perceived utility of content. Not only is the intitial cost of a color teletext receiver substantially lower (about $200 more than a regular color TV set in England) than the cost of a viewdata set (about $1,000 more than a regular color set), but, as Chapter 1 indicated, viewdata systems such as Prestel also involve charges for the use of the computer, the use of the telephone, and the viewing of certain pages of information, whereas the use of teletext pages involves only the cost of the electricity to operate the television set.

In addition to differences in cost of use, teletext systems are presently able to reach millions of users simultaneously without significant additional costs in hardware. For several hundred thousand dollars, the equipment for a teletext system can be added to regular television broadcasting equipment. But such is not the case for interactive viewdata systems like Prestel. With

19 mini-computers linked together in a nationwide network, the Prestel system could handle only 1609 users at any one time in early 1981. To accommodate hundreds of thousands, or millions, of simultaneous users would required a vast network of such computers at a cost of millions, even billions, of dollars. Until this kind of investment is made by governments and/or corporations, teletext seems to be an eminently more practical medium for the electronic delivery of printed news to *mass* audiences than does viewdata.

In addition to financial advantages for both the sender and receiver of news, teletext systems in the United Kingdom, the Netherlands, and the United States have centralized editorial control that helps to eliminate duplication of information and simplifies the means of obtaining content on the system. Centralized editorial control also enhances the continuity and quality of the news available on a teletext system, and gives the system a more well-defined "personality" than does the "common carrier" philosophy of a viewdata system such as Prestel, where the individual information providers are responsible for the news content of the system.[5] Teletext technology also enables pages of information to be updated while the viewer watches, whereas with the viewdata technology employed by the Prestel system, pages must be requested repeatedly to contain the latest updates.

At some point in the future, however, the boundaries may well begin to blur. Even though one-way teletext systems will never have the interactive capability of viewdata systems, many more pages of news and information

---

[5]For a comparison of the "personality" of the Viewtron viewdata system in the United States with the Prestel viewdata system in England, see Philip Meyer, "Emerging Opportunities in Electronic Technology: What Can We Learn from Newspapers," *VIDEOTEX '81: International Conference & Exhibition* (Middlesex, United Kingdom: Online Conferences, 1981), pp. 229–238. Meyer argues that Prestel as a whole lacks the coherence which an editor could give it, whereas Viewtron has a personality because of consistent visual appeal and the dialogue with users maintained by its editor. It should be noted that some of the largest information providers to Prestel are not altogether pleased with its common carrier policy because they believe that "high quality" information is needed to sell more Prestel TV sets. And Richard Hooper, director of Prestel, in changing the marketing strategy for Prestel from a "shotgun" (all things to all people) to a "rifle-shot sectorised 'hard sell' approach," has said that the information on Prestel must be upgraded and geared more to businesses to sell more Prestel sets, at least for the next few years. According to Peter Stothard of *The Sunday Times* (25 January 1981, p. 61), Hooper "is prepared to abandon what was a key tenet of Prestel: access for any provider of information, whatever information he wants to provide." But in a personal interview with Hooper on March 16, 1981, this writer and Professor Jay Blumler of Leeds University were told that "Prestel indexes information impartially regardless of the size of the pocketbook of the information provider" and that Hooper is still "very keen on a common carrier philosophy for Prestel." And Hooper argued in this interview that one of the strengths of Prestel over other videotex systems was "a bed rock of more general information" for specialists to explore.

could be available on teletext systems if more than two lines in the vertical blanking interval of a TV signal were used, if an entire channel on cable television were used, and if receivers' TV sets had memories that could store thousands of pages sent over the air or by cable for instant retrieval by the viewer. Such developments would increase the potential "newshole" of teletext systems enormously, and would make such systems more similar to viewdata systems in volume of news and information that could be carried, if not in interactive capabilities. Cable penetration is expected to reach the 30% level in the United States by the end of 1982, and by the end of the 1980s about half the nation's households are expected to be cable subscribers,[6] so "cable teletext" is quite possible in this country as a mass news medium within the next decade, even though the news stories it carries are likely to be very brief, just as they are on many viewdata systems today.

CHOICE OF NEWS

Even though teletext and viewdata allow the viewer to be more selective in choice of news than do other electronic media, this choice is very limited at present when compared to the choice offered by full-sized newspapers. And teletext and viewdata systems generally do not offer news stories with as much detail as do regular television news broadcasts.

As mentioned earlier, teletext systems in Great Britain and elsewhere usually offer viewers 20 or fewer general news stories of 75 to 85 words each at any given time. The same is generally true for the Prestel viewdata system, even though this system consists of nearly 200,000 pages at present, compared to 400 or so for each teletext system. A comparison of teletext news content with that of the BBC evening television news broadcast and seven newspapers (four full-sized and three tabloids) during one week day not dominated by any one or two news stories, reveals that the BBC's Channel 1 evening television news broadcast supplied from 48 to 400 words (with an average of 260 words) for eight stories carried by the Ceefax and Oracle teletext services, whereas the teletext services supplied from 34 to 88 (with an average of 66) words for each story. The tabloid newspapers carried from 90 to 820 words per story (average 287), and the full-sized papers devoted from 20 to 835 words per story (average 403). (See Table 5.1) These word counts show that the teletext systems each offered about one-fourth as may words in each news story, on the average, as did the BBC1 evening television news and the tabloid newspapers, and about one-sixth as many words per story as did the full-sized newspapers, although the lengths of stories varied greatly in the TV news program and in the newspapers.

---

[6]Harry F. Waters et al., "Cable TV: Coming of Age," *Newsweek*, August 24, 1981, p. 45.

TABLE 5.1
Comparison of Teletext, Television, and Newspaper News
in Great Britain, January 30, 1981

	ITV Oracle Teletext	BBC Ceefax Teletext	BBC 1 Evening TV News	Daily Mail (tabloid)	The Sun (tabloid)
Overall number of news stories:	10	13	16	56	60
Average number of words in those news stories carried by Teletext:	76	62	260 (n = 8)	448 (n = 3)	146 (n = 3)

	Daily Star (tabloid)	The Times	The Guardian	Yorkshire Post	Yorkshire Evening Post
Overall number of news stories:	30	100	85	80	80
Average number of words in those news stories carried by Teletext:	225 (n = 1)	457 (n = 3)	637 (n = 3)	469 (n = 3)	121 (n = 4)

Even more striking than the differences in numbers of words per news story are the differences in numbers of news stories supplied by the various media. On the day studied, the Oracle teletext system offered 10 general news stories, the Ceefax teletext system 13, the BBC Channel 1 TV news 16, the tabloid papers from 30 to 60, and the full-sized newspapers from 80 to 100. These differences clearly illustrate that the choice of news offered to teletext viewers at present in England is indeed very limited when compared to the choice offered by both tabloid and full-sized newspapers. These comparisons also suggest that teletext systems are not providing added depth or detail to the regular television news broadcasts. Even though the BBC TV news typically consists of only a few more stories than does teletext news, the regular TV news stories tend to be four times as long as the teletext stories and are often accompanied by film or videotape depicting the people, places, and events in the news. Whether these patterns will change in the future is not clear, but at present there is no great incentive to expand the news coverage of teletext and viewdata systems until these systems command significantly larger audiences and, in the case of commercial operations, until they generate substantial revenues from advertising and user fees.

The one notable exception to these very brief teletext news stories is found on Channel 2 of BBC television, where the Ceefax system regularly offers longer, less timely background news stories that are contained on "extended pages" of usually four to six screens in length. These "extended pages" constantly change screens every 15 or 20 seconds without any signal from the viewer. Thus if a person requests a certain teletext page on BBC2, he or she may get screen 3 of a six-screen extended page, then screen 4, screen 5, screen 6, screen 1, screen 2, etc. As Table 5.2 indicates, this "extended page" device enables longer news stories (usually 200 to 400 words) to be carried on teletext without extra button-pushing by the viewer, but because the viewer may enter the page at any screen, each screen must be a fairly self-contained unit. Table 5.2 shows that the "extended page" device enabled the BBC's Ceefax teletext system to provide far more news about the launching of the American space shuttle Columbia than did the ITV's Oracle teletext system or *The Guardian* newspaper (nearly 2600 words as compared to 150 words on Oracle and 550 words in *The Guardian*). Ceefax was also able to provide 10 drawings illustrating the operation and flight sequence of the space shuttle, as compared to no illustrations on Oracle and three photographs in *The Guardian*.

On a day when only one or two news stories dominate, then, it is possible for the Ceefax teletext system, through its "extended pages" to provide as much or more detail and depth in coverage as do newspapers. It is still questionable, however, whether this coverage is as easy to read as it is in newspapers, and it is definitely true that it takes considerably longer to read than in newspapers because of the time involved in selecting pages and waiting for each screen of an extended page to change.

Thus at present teletext and viewdata seen useful mainly as quick surveillance news media to acquaint viewers briefly with the latest top news stories, but not terribly useful for providing depth or details (except in the case of a dominant news story such as the launching of the space shuttle). The choice of news offered viewers by most present teletext and viewdata systems is usually very limited when compared to the choice offered by full-sized quality newspapers. Audience use patterns of both teletext and viewdata suggest that increases in the news capacities of these systems are likely to be in the *number* of stories rather than in the average length. As a recent report from the Swedish Commission on New Information Technology put it, "Most of the editorial matter of the press is not suited today for publication in videotex: it quite simply cannot be accommodated in a readable manner on a videotex page comprising about 80 words. Many pages in succession will hardly be read."[7]

---

[7]The Commission on New Information Technology, *New Media: Broadcast Teletext, Videotex* (Stockholm, Sweden: The Swedish Ministry of Education and Culture, 1981), p. 23 of the English language version of the summary of the final report translated by John Hogg.

NATURE OF NEWS

Teletext and viewdata news at present tends to be very "event-oriented" and thus not likely to probe complex issues and processes in depth. There is also a tendency on teletext and viewdata not to carry various arguments related to controversial matters, but instead to report what happens rather than what's said.

Many of the news executives and journalists I interviewed have stressed that teletext and viewdata news was concerned with "just the facts" and that it was "simple journalism." One teletext journalist said, "We're concerned with what happens, not with what's said." This journalist argued that teletext was not as susceptible to "orchestrated campaigns" as are other news media because teletext sticks to the "bare facts of what happened" rather than trying to report the various arguments associated with hotly debated issues. Another journalist, working for the Oracle system, said that this medium normally doesn't report "human interest" or court news, and sometimes tends to be "too serious." Others called teletext news "hard," meaning that it deals with timely events rather than less timely ideas or ongoing processes.

Despite the fact that teletext and viewdata systems rely upon television for reaching their audiences, the news carried on these systems is not visually oriented, as is regular television news, and therefore there are somewhat different criteria for what is deemed newsworthly by television journalists and by videotex journalists, with the former often being more interested in subjects than can be illustrated on film or videotape and the latter being more interested in timeliness and speed. As one Oracle news editor put it, "It's a fallacy that television is keen on speed. It's really more keen on what can be illustrated." The emphasis on speed among teletext and viewdata journalists means that one is likely to find far more stories on these systems dealing with "breaking events" (such as accidents and disasters, strikes and industrial actions, the jailing of accused murderers, etc.) than with "softer news" (such as personality profiles, explanations of ongoing processes or controversies, humorous happenings, etc.).

Several teletext journalists argued that teletext news could counter "the instant public theatre" of television news by providing written accounts to explain what the TV camera illustrates, but in most cases the teletext stories consist of about one-fourth the number of words used in the same television news stories, leaving little opportunity for doing more than repeating the basic facts. Even though one Dutch teletext journalist maintained that he tries "to put some perspective into teletext news stories and not just give the readers a list of facts," it is not easy in practice to provide any kind of perspective in 75 to 85 words or less. Yet, another argument advanced by this same journalist was that "people need written information to fully grasp what they hear and see on radio and television, and teletext provides this information free of charge." Another person working for the Dutch

TABLE 5.2
Comparison of Teletext and Newspaper Coverage
Of Space Shuttle and Brixton Riots
in Great Britain, April 12–13, 1981

	ITV Oracle Teletext	BBC Ceefax Teletext	The Guardian (April 13)
Number of news stories about space shuttle or Brixton riots:	7	13 (plus 10 graphics)	13 (plus 10 photos and one map)
Average number of words in these stories:	81	193	683
Number of words devoted to these news stories:			
1. Space shuttle cleared for take-off:	72	—	—
2. Shuttle takes off:	78	71	550 (3 photos)
3. Shuttle crew and trainees:	—	309 (4 screens)	—
4. Shuttle delay:	—	218 (4 screens)	—
5. Shuttle as work horse:	—	432 (7 screens) (4 graphics)	—
6. Flight sequence:	—	347 (6 screens) (6 graphics)	—
7. Shuttle problems:	—	230 (3 screens)	—
8. War in space:	—	311 (4 screens)	—

TABLE 5.2 *(continued)*
Comparison of Teletext and Newspaper Coverage
Of Space Shuttle and Brixton Riots
in Great Britain, April 12–13, 1981

	ITV Oracle Teletext	BBC Ceefax Teletext	The Guardian (April 13)
9. Beyond Columbia:	—	267 (4 screens)	—
10. In-flight reports:	—	(19 screens, averaging 21.5 words each)	—
11. London rioters glad:	86	—	—
12. Police, citizens hurt:	85	70	675, 600 (pictures)
13. Police tactics:	85	—	350, 575
14. Car search sparks violence: (timetable of events)	83	—	900 (4 photos)
15. History of Brixton tension:	78	—	390, 240, 1265, 860
16. Riot enquiry: (why did it happen?)	—	84	1400, 500, 575 (2 photos)
17. Riot preplanned?	—	70	—
18. Area devastated:	—	82	(3 photos, 1 map)

teletext system argued that the written information provided by teletext, even if no more than a basic listing of facts, was especially useful for the deaf and hard-of-hearing who suffer "terrible isolation" in this age of electronic media.

In addition to being extremely "event oriented" and brief, there seems to be some tendency for viewdata news to be somewhat less controversial than other kinds of news. Two of the journalists working for the Birmingham *Post* and *Mail's* Viewtel system (the major provider of news to the Prestel viewdata system in England) claimed that "fairly innocuous stories can draw much greater reaction on the television screen than they would in print." One example cited was a story about an English clergyman who had admitted being a homosexual. The Viewtel journalists decided not to use this story because they thought their viewers might object to its being carried on the Prestel system. It must be kept in mind, however, that the Prestel system at present is mainly a commercial information system used primarily by businessmen, and this may well lead to a more conservative, or more focused, treatment of news on this particular system. Whether this would be true on other videotex systems is not clear.

Because of the "common carrier" policy of Prestel and some other viewdata systems (the practice of leasing pages to any information provider), one executive argued that such systems could include very unorthodox views due to "the policy of indexing information impartially regardless of the size of the pocketbook of the information provider." He compared Prestel to an "electronic bookstall" where the viewer should be able to find many different sources of information and points of view, but he acknowledged that at present he didn't know of any radically different perspectives on Prestel, and he speculated that persons with greatly differing views might not be very much interested in reaching a limited audience of primarily businessmen. The Prestel system is under pressure, however, from some of the leading information providers to take a more active role in upgrading the "quality" of the information available on the system, rather than leaving questions of content up to the individual information providers, as is now the case with a "common carrier" policy. If the Post Office does get involved in making judgments about the quality of the information carried on the system, this could discourage the presentation of highly unorthodox or controversial perspectives in news and other kinds of information available via viewdata.

AUDIENCE REACTIONS

Audience research on teletext and viewdata systems suggests that the demand for news by users is very high as compared to other kinds of content, and the teletext users are generally satisfied with the systems in England and the Netherlands.

There has not been much audience research concerning videotex systems, primarily because of the very small numbers of persons using these systems until recently, however two studies of teletext users in the United Kingdom and the Netherlands—and page usage data recorded by the Prestel viewdata computers—suggest that general news pages are the most frequently accessed content of both English and Dutch teletext systems, and among the most frequently requested pages on the Prestel viewdata system.

A survey of 609 owners and renters of Philips teletext TV sets in England during 1979 and 1980 by Philips Electronics Consumer Market Research Department indicates that news, sport, and television listings are the most popular teletext pages, and more than one-third of those surveyed would like *more* news on teletext, especially news about local events. And a fall 1980 series of surveys of 227 Dutch teletext users conducted by the Audience Research Department of the Netherlands Broadcasting Foundation (NOS) indicates that the news pages of the Dutch teletext system are the most frequently viewed and the most appreciated of all the pages on the system, especially the latest news bulletins and the domestic news stories. In addition, Prestel usage data shows that on Viewtel 202 (the largest provider of news to the British viewdata system), the most popular pages are those that contain national and sports news, and these pages are also among the most often requested of the nearly 200,000 pages on the entire Prestel system.[8]

The Philips study found that in a typical week, the average British teletext user takes advantage of the service 77 times and spends almost 2 hours watching pages, suggesting that even though the news pages are the most frequently sought, the total time spent with teletext is not great (more than half of the teletext viewers were heavy viewers of television in general—they watched more than 30 hours each week). In addition to news, sports and television information are next most in demand by British teletext users. Dutch teletext viewers are most likely to view weather and traffic information, sports, and broadcasting schedules after the general news pages. These findings are consistent with those of a number of newspaper readership studies in the United States, including a 1979 Simmons nationwide study that showed that general news had the highest readership in newspapers, followed by sports and television listings. Apparently content preferences do cut across media and often across national boundaries.[9]

Both English and Dutch teletext users were quite satisfied with their respective systems, according to the Philips and NOS surveys. In England,

---

[8]My thanks to Mr. Michael Imms of the Video Division of Philips Electronics for kindly providing some of the findings from the Philips survey of owners and renters of teletext TV sets in the United Kingdom, and to Dr. Harold de Bock for taking the time to translate many of the findings of NOS surveys of Dutch teletext users. The information on Prestel usage patterns was provided in personal interviews with John Foxton, marketing manager of Viewtel, the viewdata service of the Birmingham *Post* and *Mail,* on February 27, 1981, and with Richard Hooper, director of Prestel, on March 16, 1981.

[9]In a telephone survey of 633 household heads in homes with and without cable television in Columbus, Ohio, and its suburbs in early 1980, Lee Becker found that the program preferences of subscribers to the Qube interactive cable TV system were not substantially different from those of subscribers to the other, more traditional cable TV systems. Becker concluded that audience members may both replace prior media habits by use of cable services as well as use these new services to supplement those existing habits, but it is not clear yet which of these effects is dominant. (See Lee B. Becker and Sheizaf Rafaeli, "Cable's Impact on Media Use: A Preliminary Report from Columbus," paper presented to the Theory & Methodology Division, Association for Education in Journalism, East Lansing, Michigan, August 1981. Becker is an associate professor in the School of Journalism, Ohio State University, Columbus, Ohio 43210.)

the majority of users said they were "very satisfied" with teletext, and only 5% regarded it as a luxury they seldom used. The Philips survey found that more than one-third of the respondents (who agreed to complete questionnaires and keep diaries of usage patterns) considered teletext "an extremely useful service which they could not do without." In the Netherlands, 68% of the respondents to the NOS survey were "very enthusiastic" about teletext, 27% were "somewhat enthusiastic," 4% were "somewhat disappointed," and only 1% were "very much disappointed." But nearly all the Dutch respondents (92%) favored fewer pages on teletext in return for a shorter waiting time between pages. The most common complaint among the English respondents to the Philips survey was interference with the broadcast signal (affecting 70%), and 44% also complained of problems with hand-held page selectors.

Taken together, these findings suggest that an executive working for the Independent Television News in London was correct when he observed that "teletext is viewed as an information medium, not an entertainment one." In addition, studies indicate that the information most preferred on both teletext and viewdata systems is general news. Teletext users seem to be generally satisfied with this new medium, and they seem to spend about as much time with it (17 minutes a day or so) as many people spend with newspapers in the United States.

MEDIA USE PATTERNS

Audience research in the Netherlands suggests that viewing teletext news can both stimulate and discourage news consumption from other media.

The NOS survey of 227 Dutch teletext users finds it is more likely that teletext news will spur the search for additional information in newspapers, radio, and television than vice versa, but the survey also suggests that viewing teletext news can lead to skipping regular radio and TV news broadcasts and not reading certain newspaper or magazine articles.

Only 18% of the Dutch respondents said they "often" turned to teletext to update information received from newspapers, radio, and television, but 36% said they "often" look for more news in newspapers, radio, and television after first receiving it via teletext. And 61% said that they had read an item in a newspaper that they probably would not have otherwise read except for seeing it first on teletext. Only 36% said the same for magazines, suggesting less overlap in content between Dutch teletext and magazines than between teletext and newspapers.

But 52% of the Dutch respondents said they had *not* read an article in a newspaper or magazine because they had seen it already on teletext, suggesting that whether teletext viewing increases or decreases print media consumption depends upon whether the reader wants to know more about the subject being written about. Likewise, 37% said they "often" skip the regular radio and television news because of their intention to read the news on teletext at a more convenient time.

These findings on videotex and the flow of news suggest that even though teletext and viewdata systems in England and the Netherlands are not providing news and information basically different from that in other public media, and even though what is provided tends to be briefer and more event-oriented than what is carried on other media (except perhaps for radio), there is nevertheless a demand for teletext and viewdata news and a general satisfaction with it on the part of teletext viewers. There is also some indication in the Netherlands that viewing teletext news can both stimulate and discourage news consumption from other public media. Whether many people will be content to rely largely on videotex news in the future, and to rely less on newspapers, television, and radio, or whether there will be only minor effects on these other media, is not clear from these findings.

What seems to be evident at this point is that substantial numbers of people will use teletext and viewdata systems to keep up with news, once these media are available through their televisions, and many of them will be fairly satisfied with just the present event-oriented "printed radio" news bulletins. In addition, the viewing of videotex news is likely to have *some* impact, either reinforcing and/or competing, on existing news media usage patterns. But unless changes are made in the news gathering practices of teletext and viewdata journalists, these new communication channels are not likely to offer much new information to the public, although they may provide at least brief, up to date accounts of news and information more conveniently and cheaply than do the other media.

In the next chapter I discuss the impact of teletext and viewdata on these other media.

6 Findings: Videotex and Other Media

Interviews with media executives and journalists, observations of teletext and viewdata systems in the United Kingdom and the Netherlands, and a review of related studies and articles suggest the following conclusions regarding the impact of teletext and viewdata systems on existing media.

PRESENT IMPACT ON OTHER MEDIA

Teletext and viewdata systems have had no noticeable impact on other media in Britain, the Netherlands, and West Germany to date. There is speculation that electronic information delivery could lead to longer, more in-depth articles in newspapers and magazines—and less emphasis on brief news bulletins and tabular material—but there appears to be no evidence to indicate that such changes are happening now.

Nearly all videotex executives and journalists agreed that their systems were highly unlikely to cause the demise of other printed or broadcast media in the foreseeable future, but some said that the printed media of the future might concentrate *more* on longer in-depth analyses, columns, editorials, and other such material than at present, and *less* on brief news bulletins, tabular material such as sports scores and stock prices, and other content that needs to be updated often and does not take up much space per unit.

Two BBC executives argued that teletext might hold some potential for news reporting, but unlike other technological developments in communication, it did not seem to be obviously superior to previous inventions. These executives maintained that many new developments in media technology are a product of a "curious kind of inter-craft relationship" between journalists and engineers, with some developments initiated by journalists and others by engineers. In the case of teletext, both seemed to agree that the engineers had assumed the lead in developing the technology, then had turned to journalists to see to its possible uses. Because of this pattern of development, and the lack of obvious advantages over other technologies such as radio and television, these executives doubted that teletext would be adopted as quickly and universally as radio, television, and color television were, and they also doubted that teletext would have as great an impact on journalistic practices and media use patterns as radio and television have had.

Several persons associated with the Prestel viewdata system thought that viewdata was likely to have its first effects on specialized printed media—such as directories of paper prices—that cost a great deal to print and are nearly out of date by the time they're published. These persons pointed out that present information providers to the Prestel system tend to be companies offering specialized information—mostly of a commercial nature such as metal prices, paper prices, share listings, job vacancies, etc.—that needs frequent updating. It is much cheaper and easier to update such information on a viewdata system such as Prestel, they argue, and if viewdata systems become widespread, they think such information eventually may not be available printed on paper.

In short, the consensus of those I interviewed in Britain, the Netherlands, and Germany was that teletext and viewdata were more likely to have their first effects on more specialized printed media rather than on more general news media such as newspapers, news magazines, television, and radio. But this conclusion was limited mainly to the *content* of these more general media rather than to their financial support.

EFFECTS ON ADVERTISING REVENUES

Although there is reasonable consensus that teletext and viewdata systems are not likely to bring about major changes in the content of the more general media such as newspapers and television in the foreseeable future, there is less agreement as to what effects teletext and viewdata might have on advertising revenues of other media, especially newspaper and magazine classified advertising income.

Even though teletext and viewdata have had no significant effects on other more traditional media to date, there is considerable uncertainty about what impact their development might have on the levels of income from advertising. Because many ads, especially classified, are a kind of specialized information that needs to be updated frequently, that takes up relatively little space per unit, and that lends itself to computerized indexing, there is considerable speculation that videotex systems (especially interactive viewdata systems) could be very well suited as vehicles for such advertising. Not only could such advertising be indexed by subject matter, as is the case in most newspapers and magazines at present, but on videotex systems it could be classified according to other variables such as age of product (in the case of automobiles or homes), location, model, price range, etc. It could also be withdrawn from the system as soon as the advertised item was sold.

Thus it appears that the nature of classified advertising is very compatible with the nature of videotex as a medium. Even though this may be so, videotex classified advertising will not replace newspaper classified ads unless videotex terminals become very widespread in a newspaper's local community (in use in two-thirds or more of the homes) and the cost of placing videotex classifieds is no higher than the cost of placing such ads in the newspaper. But for videotex to become such a widespread medium, the cost of it must drop dramatically, especially for viewdata systems with nearly unlimited page capacity. As indicated earlier, it is more likely that broadcast teletext systems will become mass media long before interactive viewdata systems, but the limited page capacity of the teletext systems—and their regional or national focus—does not suggest that they will become major vehicles for local classified advertising in the way that newspapers presently are, although they may carry some national classifieds in the same manner as magazines do now.

Even though the Prestel viewdata system is national in nature, it is possible for viewdata systems to be very locally oriented, as illustrated by Knight-Ridder Newspapers' Viewtron experiment in Coral Gables, Florida. This system featured local news reporting and local advertising, as well as national and international news from the Associated Press. But even with a locally oriented viewdata system, cost is probably the most important barrier to widespread use. The viewers in the Knight-Ridder Viewtron experiment did not have to pay for their videotext terminals and use of them, but beginning in 1983 users will have to pay—probably at least 30 dollars a month as compared to less than 10 dollars for the newspaper.

For the cost of viewdata receivers and use to decline to the point where viewdata penetration of households would rival newspaper penetration, most informed sources agree that subsidization is needed from advertising, TV set manufacturers, telephone or cable companies, government, or some combination thereof. The problem is that advertisers and TV set manufacturers (and probably telephone and cable companies) won't be as greatly interested in investing huge sums of money in viewdata systems until they are reasonably convinced that viewdata will become a mass medium, but viewdata is not likely to become a mass medium unless this money is forthcoming to lower the cost to the individual user—the classic "chicken and egg" problem.

It may be that viewdata systems will develop initially as regional or national services reaching special interest users who are attractive to regional or national advertisers, rather than to local ones. If this happens, and national systems such as CompuServe and The Source in the U.S. suggest it may, then certain kinds of specialized magazine advertising could be affected by viewdata advertising before general interest newspaper advertising is.

In addition to cost to the user, another problem with the development of interactive viewdata systems as mass media is the computer hardware needed to handle tens of thousands of simultaneous users. As noted in Chapter 5, during the time of this study the Prestel viewdata system had 19 minicomputers located within a local telephone call from most homes in the United Kingdom. These computers had the capability of serving up to 400 simultaneous users each, so the system could theoretically handle 7600 users at the same time. In actuality, however, the Prestel system was geared to handle only about 1600 at any one time. Although there are ways to increase the number of users, such as using television receivers with memories to store viewdata pages so that some page searching can be done "off-line" (not connected to the viewdata computer) or making some users wait until a "port" (computer hookup) is available, the fact remains that accommodating tens or hundreds of thousands of simultaneous users is a major problem for viewdata systems, but not for teletext systems that use the regular broadcast TV signal.

All this is not to say that viewdata systems will never become as widespread as daily newspapers and network television, but only that there are major problems to overcome in terms of computer hardware systems and user costs before this can happen. And even if these problems are solved, there are difficulties in reading text from a TV screen and in finding the desired material. But until teletext and viewdata systems achieve levels of local and/or specialized audience penetration that is roughly comparable to those the various printed media now have, these systems are not likely to cut significantly into the advertising revenues of the printed media. It is possible that videotext systems will create and reach audiences not covered well by any present printed or broadcast media, but this development would not necessarily have a major effect on advertising revenues going to the more traditional media.

Yet another problem with advertising on videotex systems is that no system of display advertising has been developed that would reach viewers who were not specifically seeking such advertising. This is not a problem for classified advertising, where readers actively seek out ads for certain products or services, but it is a problem for those display advertisers who want to influence people who are not necessarily seeking information about certain products or services.

At present, the Oracle teletext system is running very short (two or three line) advertising messages at the bottom of some news pages, with no illustrations. Some of the pages on Prestel also carry messages prompting other pages or services, but these are also very short and lack the visual impact of newspaper, television, and magazine ads. One of the persons I interviewed at the Dutch teletext headquarters in Hilversum suggested that a way to impose ads upon people in the same way that newspapers, magazines, and television presently do would be for a 5 or 10-second ad to appear each time a person requested another page of a teletext or viewdata system, but he did not advocate this procedure. And it seems highly unlikely that such a system would be seriously considered at a time when there is such concern over making videotext systems easy to use and attractive to potential users.

In spite of these problems, both classified and display ads appear on nearly one-half of the 28 operating electronic news delivery systems in the United States included in Linda Zaradich's fall 1981 survey.[1] Zaradich found that two of the four broadcast teletext systems, seven of the 14 cable systems, and two of the three viewdata systems offered classified ads. Display ads were carried by two of the teletext systems, eight of the cable systems, and two of the viewdata systems.

The only noticeable impact of videotext on present media advertising seems to be the tendency for some teletext users to switch from ordinary TV viewing to teletext to avoid watching televised advertising. Because teletext users are still a small fraction (about one-eightieth) of all television viewers in the United Kingdom, this is not a major factor in estimating audiences for television ads, but it could become so if teletext becomes truly widespread.

The Prestel viewdata system has had even less impact on the usage patterns and advertising revenues of traditional printed and broadcast media than has teletext because Prestel is mainly used by business people (87% of the Prestel users are so classified), and the information carried on the nearly 200,000 pages of Prestel is mostly commercial in nature. The largest group of users of Prestel are travel agents, followed by investment firms, computers and electronics companies, educational institutions, property and real estate firms, and publishing organizations. Richard Hooper, director of Prestel at the time of this study, maintained that the domestic market had not been abandoned, but he did not expect Prestel to really take hold of the residential market until "the last half of the 1980s." With about 10,000 Prestel TV sets nationwide, advertisers in the UK are not likely to be drawn to Prestel, except those that want to reach a select group of businesses.

Notwithstanding the problems associated with videotex advertising, many are taking it very seriously. The Swedish Commission on New Information Technology, in a recent report on new media, concluded:

---

[1]Linda J. Zaradich, "Electronic News Delivery: A Survey of 35 Projects," School of Journalism and Center for New Communications, Indiana University, Bloomington, October 1981.

The press is not threatened by the new media as regards the editorial contents of newspapers. The new media can supplement but not replace the paper-bound newspaper.

Advertising in videotex should be prohibited in the view of the majority of members of the Commission, as it might entail so great a loss of advertising revenue as to threaten the economy of the press.[2]

George Kennedy, in a recent article on British videotex, writes that those who are involved with it in Britain "are inclined to agree that the new medium won't revolutionize the reporting of the news, but they predict strong effects on the business side of newspapers."[3] Kennedy notes that the profit margins of British newspapers are narrower than those in the U.S., and cites several British editors as confirming that "a loss of 10% of classified advertising alone would make losers of half the local papers in Britain."[4]

In short, then, there is more uncertainty about the possible effects of videotex advertising on the revenues of existing media than about the effects of videotex content on the content of the more traditional broadcast and printed media. But even if teletext and viewdata systems do not become mass media, it is still possible for them to have significant effects on the advertising revenue of some more specialized broadcast and printed media. There are major technological and marketing problems to overcome, however, before videotex systems of any kind will have significant effects on existing media.

CONTROL OF TELETEXT AND VIEWDATA

The degree to which existing media will be able to control and profit from teletext and viewdata systems varies considerably by country. In most countries, newspapers have a better chance of operating or contributing to viewdata systems than do broadcast teletext systems. Television organizations, on the other hand, seem to have more potential opportunities with broadcast teletext systems.

In Finland, the largest newspaper is one of three organizations that own and run the viewdata system. In the Netherlands, VNU (an organization of publishers) has its own viewdata system. In West Germany, there has been considerable conflict between the newspaper industry and the broadcasters over who has the right to publish information on viewdata and teletext services. Both Germany and Sweden have legal definitions as to what con-

---

[2]Commission on New Information Technology, *New Media: Broadcast teletext, videotex* (Stockholm, Sweden: The Swedish Ministry of Education and Culture, 1981).

[3]George P. Kennedy, "British videotex experience gives hint of future," *presstime* (journal of the American Newspaper Publishers Association), September 1981, p. 15.

[4]*Ibid.*

stitutes broadcasting, and these definitions may prohibit newspaper companies from becoming directly involved with TV-based services such as teletext and viewdata. In the United Kingdom, several regional (provincial) newspapers are presently supplying news, weather, and travel information to the Prestel viewdata system run by the British Post Office, but so far none of the large national daily newspapers such as *The Guardian, The Times,* or *The Daily Telegraph* have been much interested in Prestel, with the exception of *The Financial Times* which provides business information through a partly-owned subsidiary company known as FINTEL.

So it seems that in Britain and elsewhere, newspapers have a better chance to get involved with viewdata systems (even if only as information providers) than with the teletext systems that tend to be controlled by the broadcasters such as the BBC or the Independent Television network. In the United States, however, some companies such as Field Enterprises own both newspapers and television stations, and thus can involve newspapers in teletext. One such experiment in the Chicago area is "Keyfax," which broadcasts from television station WFLD (owned by Field Enterprises) and uses information from the Chicago *Sun-Times,* also owned by Field Enterprises.

A survey of 28 operating and seven planned electronic home news delivery systems in the United States by Linda Zaradich suggests that only about one-fifth of the news on broadcast teletext systems comes from newspapers, whereas about three-fifths of the news on cable and telephone viewdata systems comes from newspapers.[5] Half of the 28 operating systems in Zaradich's fall 1981 survey were cable news systems that offered no selectivity to the user. Even without selectivity, it is clear from the survey that these cable news systems were the most common, the most local in nature, and the most likely to be operated by newspapers.

This upsurge in cable news systems may mean that broadcasters will not retain control of teletext systems to the extent that they do today. Cable teletext (one-way systems with thousands of pages of information) could develop as a medium somewhere between broadcast teletext (with only a few hundred pages) and full-fledged interactive viewdata systems. Newspapers owning cable companies, or leasing channels from such companies, could transmit a revolving set of pages of news, weather, sports, financial information, advertising, etc. through the cable in the same manner that broadcasters now send these pages with broadcast TV signals in such systems as Ceefax and Oracle. The viewer would be able to select only the pages of interest, unlike most of the present cable news systems where one must wait until certain pages appear on the screen. As pointed out in Chapter 5, cable penetration is expected to reach the 30% level in the United

---

[5]Zaradich, *op. cit.,* pp. 5-6.

States by the end of 1982, and by the end of the 1980s about half the nation's households are expected to be cable subscribers, so cable teletext is a real possibility for many U.S. newspapers in the next decade.[6]

Newspapers that are getting involved with teletext or viewdata systems—simple nonselective, one-way selective, or two-way interactive—are doing so for two major reasons: (1) To "protect their territory" and thus prevent other companies from threatening their advertising revenues, especially classified ad income; and (2) To promote their printed paper, much as they are beginning to do via other media such as radio, television, and billboards. Apparently this is not confined to the United States. One teletext executive in the Netherlands opposed letting the Dutch newspapers get involved with the Dutch teletext system on the grounds that the newspapers used pages on the viewdata system primarily for promotion and not for what he called "real information." He claimed this has also happened in West Germany, and he argued that it was not "freedom of information" to make the public pay for public affairs news.

In addition to protecting turf and promoting themselves, there is evidence from the Zaradich survey that many U.S. newspapers involved with videotex systems are tying advertising on these systems to advertising in the printed paper by offering discounts for advertisers who buy ads in both media.[7] Of 23 newspapers involved with videotex and offering classified or display advertising, 12 offered discounts for ads run in both the newspaper and the videotex system, and one paper refused to sell ads on videotex unless they were also purchased for publication in the printed newspaper. One paper offering a discount on display ads planned to charge three dollars per repetition (minimum 10 repetitions) for display ads run in both the newspaper and the cable news system, and 100 dollars per repetition (minimum 50) for ads run on the system only, thus strongly discouraging the purchase of advertising for the cable system only. Many of the U.S. newspapers getting involved with videotex systems seem determined to use these systems to maintain or increase the advertising revenue from the printed paper as well to make extra income from advertising on the electronic systems.

NEWS VERSUS OTHER INFORMATION

The development of teletext and viewdata systems will probably contribute to blurring the distinction between news and other kinds of information, including advertising, on these systems.

Present teletext and viewdata systems, except perhaps for Knight-Ridder Newspapers' Viewtron experiment, seem to have little social or political

---

[6]Harry F. Waters et al., "Cable TV: Coming of Age," *Newsweek*, August 24, 1981, p. 45.
[7]Zaradich, *op. cit.*, pp. 8–45.

identity in the same way that many newspapers have had. As Rex Winsbury put it in his thoughtful study of the British Prestel viewdata system: "The idea of a social and political role is central to newspapers, foreign to computers. Pure electronic communication is central to computers, foreign to newspapers."[8] This seems especially true for viewdata systems such as Prestel, where all kinds of information is available, from accounting standards to zinc price movements. As pointed out earlier, most of the information available from Prestel is commercial in nature, not social or political. Most of this information consists of facts and figures, not accounts of events designed to inform and educate the viewer.

Because of the multitude of information providers (about 500) to a "common carrier" viewdata system such as Prestel, the system has no distinguishable editorial policy or political identity and no interest in crusading for social or political reforms in the same way that many newspapers would have. One executive associated with Prestel argued that its users were not much interested in *who* provides the information carried on its pages, but rather in *what* facts appeared on those pages.

As mentioned earlier, Philip Meyer made this same point when he wrote that a newspaper enhanced the value of its advertising space "by making itself a credible, heeded, respected voice in the community" and thus being able to deliver "influence along with the information."[9] As Meyer put it, "Our product is both information and the context of information, and it takes an editorial side to shape that context into an aesthetic and influential package."[10] Meyer noted that part of the appeal of videotex technology is that it may increase the opportunities for the delivery of specialized information, but he questioned whether videotex can also deliver influence along with that information. To Meyer, "Prestel's role (and presumably that of other similar viewdata systems) is more that of a neutral broker of information than maintainer of community beliefs and values."[11] But Meyer argued that teletext and viewdata systems that have a strong editor, such as Knight-Ridder's Viewtron experiment did, may have significant influence potential.

Meyer's observations suggest that there is a distinction between news and other kinds of information—that journalistic traditions and values are not entirely compatible with the business and commercial nature of most videotex systems, or at least that such systems are not likely to have the credibility and influence attributed to many journalistic organizations. Because many videotex systems are primarily concerned with selling infor-

---

[8]Rex Winsbury, *The Electronic Bookstall: Push-button Publishing on Videotex* (London: International Institute of Communications, 1979), p. 67.

[9]Philip Meyer, "Emerging Opportunities in Electronic Technology: What We Can Learn from Newspapers," *VIDEOTEX '81: International Conference & Exhibition* (Middlesex, United Kingdom: Online Conferences, 1981), p. 233.

[10]*Ibid.*

[11]*Ibid.*, p. 234.

mation as a commodity, rather than ferreting out the truth or exposing injustices, the boundaries between journalistic information (news) and more commercial kinds of information (advertising) that have been maintained in the more traditional media by various devices (labeling ads as such, signing news stories and editorials, etc.) may break down considerably in these systems, much to the detriment of journalistic values and credibility.

In short, getting more into the "information business" with videotex systems and less into the "news business" may mean that fewer critical controversial news stories and editorials will be available through these systems than through the more traditional printed and broadcast media. Journalistic values may take even more of a back seat to commercial interests in videotex systems than they do in many present-day media.

REGULATION

Involvement with teletext and viewdata could lead to increased government regulation of printed media, especially newspapers, in societies such as the United States and the United Kingdom where there has been traditionally very little such regulation.

Because teletext and viewdata are electronic media, and because electronic media have been regulated more by the government in many countries than have printed media, newspapers and other printed media that operate or contribute to teletext and viewdata systems may find themselves subject to a number of government regulations that once applied only to broadcasters or to telephone or cable companies.

In the case of teletext, which makes use of the regular broadcast TV signal, the same regulations applying to television broadcasting (such as the fairness doctrine and the equal time provision of the 1934 Communications Act in the United States) might very well apply to broadcast teletext systems, whether or not such systems were owned and operated by newspapers or broadcasters. Although the predominant mood in Washington, D.C., is now one of de-regulation rather than regulation, the Federal Communications Commission will probably be involved at least in licensing teletext systems, if not in regulating their content. The FCC may also allocate several vertical blanking lines, or even full broadcast channels, to teletext services. Although unlikely, the FCC could also characterize teletext as a common carrier, so that the licensee would have to accept information from all those wishing to put it on the system and could not itself provide information.[12]

---

[12]Joseph Grundfest & Stuart N. Brotman, *Teletext and Viewdata: The Issues of Policy, Service, and Technology* (New York, N.Y.: Aspen Institute for Humanistic Studies, 1979), pp. 51–52.

Some unanswered questions about teletext regulation include: Should the current licensee of the associated TV station be permitted to offer a teletext service or would separate owners be advisable? How long would a term of license be? Should a spectrum fee be charged? What criteria should be used to select the teletext licensees and to determine whether their licenses should be renewed? Should persons who are prohibited from owning a newspaper and broadcast facility in the same community also be prohibited from owning a teletext system?[13]

In the United Kingdom and the Netherlands, there appear to be fewer questions about the regulation of teletext than in the United States because the teletext services in these countries are operated by the traditional national broadcasting organizations (the British Broadcasting Corporation, the Independent Television Network, and the Netherlands Broadcasting Foundation), and teletext services are subject to the same regulations governing these broadcasting organizations.

In the case of viewdata systems, which make use of the telephone or a cable system for linking the television set to a computer, regulations applying to telecommunications and data-processing services might well apply to these systems, regardless of their ownership. In the United States, the FCC has historically exercised regulatory oversight over telecommunications services (largely those provided by the American Telephone and Telegraph Company, the largest such organization), but it has not exercised authority over data-processing services. In recent years, as computers have been linked to telephone networks to transmit data, the boundaries between the two services have become blurred—resulting in the coining of the term "compunications" (a combination of "computer" and "communications").[14] So Congress and the FCC were faced with finding a workable distinction between communications and data processing.

In April of 1981, the FCC, in its Computer II Inquiry, decided to divide the telephone industry into two parts by distinguishing between *basic service* (local and long distance calls) and *enhanced service* (data processing, data transmission, and anything else combining computers with telephones). Although basic telephone services were to continue to be regulated by the FCC, enhanced services were deregulated and left wide open for market entry and competition. Everyone, including AT&T, could offer enhanced services without FCC approval. But AT&T would have to offer such enhanced services through a separate subsidiary with separate accounting

[13]Edwina E. Dowell, "Electronic Home News Delivery: Journalistic and Public Policy Implications," in John W. Ahlhauser, ed., *Electronic Home News Delivery: Journalistic and Public Policy Implications* (Bloomington, Indiana: School of Journalism and Center for New Communications, Indiana University, 1981), p. 18.

[14]Although the creation of the term "compunications" is uncertain, it has been attributed to Professor Anthony Oettinger's team of Harvard University researchers.

systems to prevent it from making unfair use of its government-sanctioned monopoly status to overwhelm others (especially existing news media) who might want to offer enhanced services via viewdata systems. There are still fears in the United States, especially among newspaper publishers, however, that AT&T could overwhelm any other competition if it were allowed to create and control the information flowing over its telephone lines, even through a separate subsidiary company.[15]

Another aspect of viewdata regulation is the role of government in ensuring privacy in viewdata systems. With a per-page billing system, the telephone or cable system will have access to large volumes of data concerning the viewing and buying habits of its users. This data could be sought by the government, the user's employer, creditors, or insurance companies, etc. The courts of the United States have held that analogous information, including bank and telephone records, can be made available to law enforcement authorities who have been granted a subpoena. Viewdata could also be used for electronic surveillance, such as intercepting messages sent by the user through the system to another user.

Still another area of possible regulation with regard to both teletext and viewdata is cross-ownership of information services. For example, a newspaper in a city may also become the dominant information provider on the viewdata system, or the owner of a cable teletext system. If cross-ownership patterns seem to be emerging that preclude others from supplying information to teletext and viewdata systems, and thus restrict diversity of views and opinions, legislation may be forthcoming.[16]

Whatever the case, it is clear that the new electronic media of teletext and viewdata pose important challenges and questions to western (particularly U.S.) definitions of freedom of the press. If videotex is viewed mainly as part of the press, this could remove it from FCC jurisdiction on the grounds that the First Amendment guards against restricting freedom of the press. In that case, any attempt to subject the new media to a broadcaster-type content review could be considered a violation of First Amendment protection of the press. In European societies, where there are no explicit "First Amendment" rights, newspapers are still afforded a traditional freedom from control, whereas broadcasting is more regulated, so the question of whether videotex is more like the press than like broadcasting is still a fundamentally important one.

Anthony Smith, in his book *Goodbye Gutenberg,* predicts that "it will be very difficult in the long run to keep these new services free from content regulation, even though the British Post Office, at the start of its Prestel service, decided to set itself against such regulation."[17] Smith points out

---

[15]Edwina E. Dowell, *op. cit.,* pp. 18–20.

[16]Joseph Grundfest and Stuart N. Brotman, *op. cit.,* pp. 44–51.

[17]Anthony Smith, *Goodbye Gutenberg: The Newspaper Revolution of the 1980s* (Oxford, England: Oxford University Press, 1980), p. 259.

that the Prestel viewdata service was set up as a "common carrier" that was not supposed to make judgments on the content being offered by various information providers, but the Post Office does reserve the right to exclude (temporarily) any material suspected of being libelous, in contempt of court, etc. The Information Provider accepts all legal responsibility for the material he places in the Post Office computer, but under British law the Post Office can be held partially liable as publisher of any offensive information. The risks of this can be reduced, however, by the Post Office taking reasonable steps to withhold such information until its legality has been tested. This, Smith predicts, could prove to be the first stepping stone towards content regulation.[18]

Treating videotex mainly as part of the press and thus exempting it from most regulation would not, however, solve the press' problems regarding electronic publishing. If other interests such as the broadcast media, telephone companies, or cable operators assume a dominant role in the ownership and operation of electronic delivery systems, and the press' role is confined to providing information for videotex systems owned and controlled by others, then newspapers would lose much of the autonomy and profits they presently enjoy by publishing the information they gather and edit and setting the final price for readers and advertisers.[19] Regulation of some kind is probably needed to keep such corporate giants as AT&T from dominating viewdata, if not teletext, systems.

This view is shared by Richard Neustadt in his book, *The Birth of Electronic Publishing,* where he advocates strict enforcement of telephone companies' obligations to provide transmission service to all without discrimination, as long as the telephone network is the only way to reach the general public with interactive videotex.[20] Neustadt also thinks it may be desirable to restrict the electronic publishing activities of common carriers such as AT&T, and to start debate on whether to require cable systems to lease channels to those who want to offer information services.

Although Neustadt generally advocates little or no government regulation of teletext and viewdata, he writes that government intervention with regard to telephone carriers and cable systems is important because it promotes freedom for publishers and diversity for audiences, making it possible for even the smallest information providers to have a chance to distribute their products and ideas to a national audience.

Thus, although there have been no significant effects on existing media

---

[18]*Ibid.*

[19]Thomas L. McPhail, *The Future of the Daily Newspaper: Public Policy Issues* (Halifax South, Nova Scotia, Canada: Institute for Research on Public Policy, 1980), pp. 66–67.

[20]Richard M. Neustadt, *The Birth of Electronic Publishing: Legal and Economic Issues in Telephone, Cable and Over the Air Teletext and Videotext* (White Plains, N.Y.: Knowledge Industry Publications, 1982).

from the new teletext and viewdata systems to date, it is fairly clear that the most significant potential effects will be in the areas of advertising revenue, the blurring of the distinction between "news" and other kinds of information, and increased government regulation of media that have long been free of most such rules. Of course, all these effects are contingent upon the widespread development and adoption of teletext and viewdata systems. If these systems are not widely used throughout any given society, their impact on other media could be minimal.

It has been argued earlier in this book that broadcast teletext is likely to develop and be adopted much more quickly than are the more expensive viewdata systems. But it is also likely that teletext will have less dramatic effects on existing media because of the limited number of pages, the lack of interactive capabilities, and the regional or national nature of many teletext systems. Thus even if teletext does become a mass, or quasi-mass, medium, its effects on other media, particularly newspapers, may be fairly minimal. At this point, the picture is still very hazy, but it should become considerably clearer in the next decade.

7 Conclusions

It is clear from this study that the longest running teletext and viewdata systems in the world are not yet unique journalistic media—(1) they do not provide much new information previously unavailable from existing media; (2) the choice and volume of news are quite limited as compared to newspapers; (3) journalists working for teletext and viewdata do very little original reporting; (4) the news that is carried on these systems tends to be superficial and event-oriented; (5) the systems themselves are not dramatically new in their appeal to different senses; (6) they have not had significant impact on other media in Britain and the Netherlands; (7) they are more difficult and expensive to use for casual reading than printed media; (8) and they (especially the more expensive viewdata receivers) are not diffusing among the public nearly as quickly as many had predicted they would.

In short, teletext and viewdata are not yet really new media, nor are they satisfactory substitutes for some of the older media. Rather, they are caught somewhere in technological limbo as they strive to carve out a niche for themselves in the existing economic and media order. The fairly minor effects they have had thus far on journalistic work are not encouraging for those interested in higher quality journalism, although they do provide more speed, convenience, and viewer choice than some previous media have, if not better news coverage. But for those who take seriously the exhortation of the Hutchins Commission that the press provide "a truthful, comprehensive, and intelligent account of the day's events in a context which gives them meaning,"[1] teletext and viewdata thus far are disappoint-

---

[1] Commission on Freedom of the Press, *A Free and Responsible Press* (Chicago: University of Chicago Press, 1947), p. 20.

ments, and they may remain so for a long time to come because of economic and technological constraints.

In spite of the present limitations of teletext and viewdata as news media, there are indications from audience surveys in Britain and the Netherlands that those who possess teletext TV sets turn to them frequently for news and are generally satisfied with what they are getting. There are also indications that viewing teletext news can both stimulate and discourage the use of other news media. Thus there is the possibility that if teletext and viewdata were to become mass media, many audience members might be satisfied with the very sketchy news accounts available from these electronic "printed radio" services.

It is not clear, however, that users of videotex systems would be willing to rely exclusively on such systems for news reports. It must be remembered that the teletext and viewdata users surveyed in Britain and the Netherlands also read newspapers, listened to radio news programs, and watched regular television news broadcasts. Their apparent satisfaction with teletext and viewdata must be considered in the context of other media use patterns. If teletext and viewdata were to replace newspapers and other media, many people might not be so satisfied with these electronic news delivery systems.

The same may be true for the journalists working for teletext and viewdata systems. Because most of them are relatively young and inexperienced, it is not possible now to know whether they would maintain the view over the years that videotex technology is either beneficial or neutral to journalists in general. And it is possible that, faced with entire careers in teletext and viewdata journalism, their present relatively low levels of job satisfaction would decline even further. But if teletext and viewdata technologies are used for news *gathering* as well as news distribution, the prospects for them to contribute positively to journalism and journalistic careers will be much brighter than they seem to be now, especially if such news gathering efforts are devoted to the collection of "general information" for a broad public.

Because viewdata systems are able to offer specialized, individualized information on hundreds of thousands of pages, they may be tempted to put a low priority on journalistic work devoted to the coverage of public affairs. Present-day broadcast teletext systems, on the other hand, seem to want to appeal to a very general, mass audience. But they are content now to rely mainly on the same information sources as those used by newspapers and TV news programs, putting the emphasis on speed of delivery and convenience rather than on the provision of different accounts of the news.

The audience studies done thus far on teletext and viewdata systems suggest that it would be a mistake for either kind of system to downplay the importance of general news. Even on the Prestel system, with nearly 200,000 pages of information, the national and international news pages supplied primarily by the Birmingham *Post & Mail* are among those most heavily accessed. The same is true for teletext systems in Britain and the Netherlands, and for the Viewtron viewdata system tested by Knight-Ridder Newspapers in Coral Gables, Florida, where national news was accessed twice as frequently as any other kind of information supplied by the Associated Press.[2] As John Wooley, editor of Viewtron put it, "These results confirm our earlier hunch that news is a critically important ingredient in a successful Viewtron system."[3]

It is important for teletext and viewdata systems to offer general news of interest to a wide public not only for keeping subscribers happy, but also for preserving a sense of community needed for democratic government. As Richard Gray, Jay Blumler, and others have pointed out so well, there must be a sense of community as well as a sense of individuality within a democracy.[4] If teletext and viewdata technology is to contribute to better journalism, as well as to better democratic forms of government, there must be an emphasis on general news as well as on specialized information. It may be true that people will not spend the money for a viewdata receiver unless the viewdata system offers specialized information and services not available elsewhere. But the data on use of pages for both Prestel and Viewtron suggest that once obtained, such systems are used very frequently to check on the latest general news of the world, the nation, and in the case of Viewtron, the local area.

Given the frequency of use of general news pages on both teletext and viewdata systems, it is unlikely that this kind of content will be eliminated from these systems, especially if they become as widespread as many are predicting. But it is highly questionable how much of this news content will be supplied from independent reporting as opposed to news agencies and reports from other media. Independent reporting costs money, and often a lot of it. This money is presently tied to circulation and the proportions of audiences reached by various media in western industrialized countries. Blumler reminds us that if viewdata systems succeed in offering specialized information to specialized audiences, this may mean a decreased share of the audience for any given content on a viewdata system, or other media channels, leading to decreased revenue to support news-gathering efforts.[5] And even if the news pages do command a significant proportion of the

---

[2]Keith Fuller, "Report of AP's Participation in Knight-Ridder Viewtron Project," Associated Press, Fall 1981, p. 2.

[3]"Viewtron Test Shows Wide Usage of AP News," *AP Log*, November 9, 1981, p. 2.

[4]Richard Gray, "Implications of the New Information Technology for Democracy," in John W. Ahlhauser, ed., *Electronic Home News Delivery: Journalistic and Public Policy Implications* (Bloomington, Indiana: School of Journalism and Center for New Communications, Indiana University, 1981), p. 73; and Jay G. Blumler, "Information Overload: Is There a Problem?" in Eberhard Witte, ed., *Human Aspects of Telecommunication* (New York: Springer-Verlag, 1980), pp. 233-35.

[5]*Ibid.*

available viewers, some way must be found for advertisers to reach these viewers, or the viewers must somehow be charged for the news they consume, for the revenues to support quality independent news reporting efforts.

The tendency of teletext and viewdata systems to rely heavily on the same news accounts as other media in Britain and the Netherlands raises the possibility that these systems will contribute to the growing technical and economic convenience of monopoly. This tendency is already apparent in the practices of teletext systems such as Ceefax and Oracle that rely so heavily on the same wire services and that use each other as news sources, thus creating a kind of "closed system" of news that is circular and mutually reinforcing in nature. But viewdata systems, with nearly unlimited numbers of pages and "common carrier" policies that would permit a wide variety of information providers at a reasonable cost, could work against monopolistic tendencies, especially if such systems were more locally oriented than those presently operating in England and the Netherlands. Viewdata systems that provide the capability for various users to send messages to one another could also work against the centralized nature of many mass communication systems, where one organization transmits information in a mostly one-way manner to audience members. There is still the possibility of some control by those who own and operate the computers for such viewdata systems, but this possibility would be greatly diminished if true common carrier policies were applied to these systems.

But if there are problems in marketing such systems, as there have been with Britain's Prestel, then there may be pressure from the large information providers to restrict access to pages to "quality" information providers—defined as those who have information that will prompt people to buy viewdata terminals and use viewdata pages. Of course, there is evidence that quality news reporting *will* prompt people to use viewdata pages, and there is no reason to doubt that they will purchase viewdata TV sets for this purpose if the price is competitive with that paid for other news media.

Thus it can be seen that in addition to the technological constraints of teletext and viewdata as news media, there are also a host of economic and political factors that interrelate in complex ways to make it quite difficult for teletext and viewdata to contribute to high quality journalism and to the functioning of democratic forms of government. Some of these limitations, although serious, are not insurmountable. Technological advances most likely will make videotex systems much easier to use than they are at present. News and other information will be organized in various ways—by key words and topics as well as by the present "tree structure" that forces the viewer to make a series of decisions to find specific stories. High resolution screens will offer many more than the present 80 or 85 words. The numbers of pages will be greatly increased on teletext systems with the use of entire cable channels. Ways will be found to incorporate advertising into commercial systems to reduce the costs to individual viewers.

But other limitations—the fragmentation and isolation of audiences, the centralized ownership and control of the systems, the reliance on fewer observers and reporters for the sake of efficiency, and the lack of portability and privacy of videotex receivers—are not as easily overcome.

Perhaps they need not be overcome if videotex is to develop as an adjunct to existing media—an add-on channel that has little impact on the other more traditional forms of mass communication. But the "principle of relative constancy" (the "fixed pie" theory) tested by Maxwell McCombs in the United States suggests that any significant gains in personal income devoted to videotex (or any other new medium) will be at the expense of other media.[6] And the studies of uses of time by urban adults in the United States in 1965 and 1975 by John Robinson document that increased time spent with television (from an average of 89 minutes a day in 1965 to 130 minutes in 1975) was associated with decreased time spent with newspapers (from 22 minutes a day to 14).[7]

Thus it is likely that if teletext and viewdata systems become widely used, other media will suffer declines in use. It is quite possible that these media will include both printed and broadcast channels, but it is difficult to project what kinds of *content* will suffer the most. Various studies of newspaper readership and videotex audiences indicate a strong interest in news, and other studies have shown moderately strong correlations between television *news* viewing and newspaper reading.[8] These findings, taken together, imply that teletext and viewdata will not have as great an impact on *news* consumption from other media as on other kinds of content.

But, as noted in Chapter 6, videotex systems may have significant impact on the economic foundations of other news media and in this manner may limit the availability and scope of alternate channels of news. Thus the

---

[6]Maxwell E. McCombs, "Mass Media in the Marketplace," *Journalism Monographs*, 24 (August 1972); and Maxwell McCombs and Chaim Eyal, "Spending on Mass Media," *Journal of Communication*, 30: 153-158 (Winter 1980).

[7]John P. Robinson, "Toward a Post-Industrious Society," *Public Opinion*, August/September, 1979. I am grateful to Philip Meyer for pointing out these specific figures in his article, "What Videotex Can Learn from Newspapers," *Nieman Reports*, Winter 1981, pp. 12-15.

[8]For a review of some of these studies, see Chapter 5 of this book and David H. Weaver and Judith M. Buddenbaum, "Newspapers and Television: A Review of Research on Uses and Effects," American Newspaper Publishers Association *News Research Report*, No. 19, April 20, 1979 (reprinted in G. Cleveland Wilhoit and Harold de Bock, eds., *Mass Communication Review Yearbook*, Volume 1 (Beverly Hills and London: Sage Publications, 1980), pp. 371-380). See also David H. Weaver, "Recent Trends in Newspaper Readership Research," *Center for New Communications Research Report* No. 5 (Bloomington, Indiana: School of Journalism, 1978).

public may have to become more dependent upon videotex for at least certain kinds of news. Whether by choice or by economic mandate, then, videotex systems may become major providers of news to the public. Because of this very real possibility, the following suggestions, based on the findings of this study, are offered for the development of videotex systems as high quality news media.

RECOMMENDATIONS

1. Teletext and viewdata journalists should be hired to *report* news as well as to edit and disseminate news gathered by others.

2. Teletext and viewdata journalists should not be isolated from other journalists in their parent organizations. Rather, they should be located in the same newsrooms with other journalists, be paid the same, and have the same status and privileges.

3. Audience surveys of teletext and viewdata users should be shared with journalists as well as managers, so that the journalists have a better idea of who their audience is, what uses are being made of their work, and what kinds of information might be supplied that is not presently offered on teletext and viewdata systems.

4. Experienced editors and reporters, as well as those relatively inexperienced, should be hired as videotex journalists. Even though many teletext and viewdata sytems are in their infancy and are not reaching large numbers of people, the quality of their content will have a bearing on how many people will become subscribers. Experienced journalists should be in charge of videotex news from the beginning, even if only as part-time workers, as in the case of Belgium, or editorial consultants.

5. News stories generally should be allowed to run as long as they need to on viewdata systems, if not on teletext. If most news stories on a system are only one page in length, users may indeed become accustomed to not reading more than 80 or 90 words per story. But if stories are allowed to run 500 to 800 words, as in quality newspapers, there is evidence from the Knight-Ridder Viewtron experiment that one-third or more of those beginning such stories will finish them. Besides, quality news reporting cannot be done in 80 or 90 words in most cases.

6. In the case of teletext, where the number of pages is presently quite limited, references to more detailed accounts of news stories in other media should be made wherever possible to encourage viewers to go beyond the bulletins provided by teletext.

7. In both teletext and viewdata systems, news content should be prominently featured in all guides and indexes to the content of the systems,

and there should be separate indexes for various kinds of news (local, national, etc.) to alert readers to all such stories carried on the system. In other words, it should be possible for a viewer to get an overview of the news content of teletext and viewdata systems by calling up only a few pages.

8. Teletext and viewdata systems should be equipped with a "Next" button that allows viewers to leaf through frames in much the same manner as one would read a newspaper—without having to request certain page numbers or return to the news indexes to check on various page numbers. This feature should allow viewers to proceed forward or backward in the systems without having to request specific page numbers, once they have requested a beginning page in the news section.

9. The cost of teletext and viewdata services should be kept as low as possible by initial subsidies from telephone, cable, and computer companies; from television set manufacturers; from the various media companies trying to develop these systems; and from government grants to develop public service information and electronic mail services. Unless viewdata services are available at low cost, there is a danger of further widening the gap between the information rich and the information poor in society.

10. There should be government legislation to prevent those who own the telephone lines and the cables from controlling the content of viewdata systems, and to require those using the public airwaves to serve the public interest as regular radio and television broadcasters are now required to do. Common carrier policies that permit a wide variety of information providers to place their messages on viewdata systems with a minimum of constraints are needed to counter the tendencies toward centralization and monopoly in the telephone, computer, and media industries.

FUTURE POSSIBILITIES FOR VIDEOTEX

These recommendations assume that teletext and viewdata will become widely used media—for general news as well as other kinds of information and services. But at this time, as indicated before, there is no assurance of widespread adoption and use, at least not in the foreseeable future. The predictions range from broadcaster Ted Turner's statement that today's newspaper will disappear within 10 years to Missouri newspaper publisher Robert White's observation that the longer he remained in the cable TV business, the less convinced he became that newspapers might be distributed via the cable.[9]

---

[9]"Turner: Electronic Papers Now" and "White: Cable Is No Threat," Inland Daily Press Association Newsletter, October 31, 1981, p. 2.

At present, newspaper information is about 20 times cheaper than the same information delivered on a viewdata system.[10] But if the costs of the newspaper and other printed media continue to escalate, and if the costs of electronic delivery systems such as teletext and viewdata continue to decline, this difference in costs could be reduced rather quickly. Also, it is fairly certain that people are not likely to buy electronic information systems solely because of their news content. Most likely, the "electronic newspaper" will be only one of many services available on a home viewdata system (games, mail, banking, shopping, reservations, etc.), and if so, people may be willing to pay considerably more for such a system than they now pay for newspapers and magazines.[11]

If general news content is to be an important component of new electronic information delivery systems—and present usage studies suggest it will be—the findings and recommendations of this study should be seriously considered. Journalism and journalists are too important to democratic forms of government to do otherwise; for good journalism, like good research, offers the possibility of creating knowledge and an informed public, not just the marketing of discrete pieces of information. As Anthony Smith puts it in the conclusion to *Goodbye Gutenberg:*

> Turning information into knowledge is the creative skill of the age, for it involves discovering ways to burrow into the abundance rather than augment it, to illuminate rather than search.[12]

The strength of the best journalistic media in this country, and around the world, has always been *content* rather than delivery. This, at least, will remain true in the era of electronic news delivery, even though great pressures to emphasize marketing rather than news gathering will exist. The findings and recommendations of this study are a reminder of the importance of substance over style, and of content over form.

---

[10]Thomas L. McPhail, *The Future of the Daily Newspaper: Public Policy Issues* (Halifax South, Nova Scotia, Canada: Institute for Research on Public Policy, 1980), p. 6.

[11]*Ibid.*; and personal interview with Richard Hooper, director of Prestel, London, March 16, 1981.

[12]Anthony Smith, *Goodbye Gutenberg: The Newspaper Revolution of the 1980s* (Oxford, England: Oxford University Press, 1980), p. 326.

Bibliography

Books and Monographs

Ahlhauser, John W., ed. *Electronic home news delivery: Journalistic and public policy Implications.* Bloomington, Ind.: School of Journalism and Center for New Communications, 1981.

Commission on Freedom of the Press. *A free and responsible press.* Chicago: University of Chicago Press, 1947.

Commission on New Information Technology, The. *New media: Broadcast teletext, videotex.* Stockholm, Sweden: The Swedish Ministry of Education and Culture, 1981. English language version translated by John Hogg.

Compaine, Benjamin M. *The newspaper industry in the 1980s: An assessment of economics and technology.* White Plains, N.Y.: Knowledge Industry Publications, 1980.

Forschungsgruppe Kammerer. *Struktur, Spektrum und Potentiale der geschäftlichen Bildschirmtext-nutzung.* Köln, 1981.

Grundfest, Joseph, & Brotman, Stuart N. *Teletext and viewdata: The issues of policy, service, and technology.* New York, N.Y.: Aspen Institute for Humanistic Studies, 1979.

Hess, Stephen. *The Washington reporters.* Washington, D.C.: The Brookings Institution, 1981.

Hynds, Ernest C. *American newspapers in the 1980s.* New York: Hastings House, 1980.

Inside Videotex: Proceedings of a seminar held March 13-14, 1980. Toronto, Canada: Infomart, 1980.

Johnstone, John, Slawski, Edward, Bowman, William. *The News People.* Urbana: University of Illinois Press, 1976.

McCombs, Maxwell E. Mass Media in the Marketplace. *Journalism Monographs, 24,* August 1972.

McPhail, Thomas L. *The future of the daily newspaper: Public policy issues.* Halifax South, Nova Scotia, Canada: The Institute for Research on Public Policy, 1980.

Money, Steve A. *Teletext and viewdata.* London and Boston: Newnes Technical Books, 1979.

117

Neustadt, Richard M. *The birth of electronic publishing.* White Plains, N.Y.: Knowledge Industry Publications, 1982.

Prestel Business Directory. October 1980.

Prestel Handbook II. June 1980.

Prestel 1980. London: Post Office Telecommunication, 1980.

Sigel, Efrem, ed. *Videotext: The coming revolution in home/office information retrieval.* New York: Harmony Books, 1980.

Smith, Anthony. *Goodbye Gutenberg: The newspaper revolution of the 1980s.* New York, Oxford: Oxford University Press, 1980.

Tunstall, Jeremy. *Journalists at work.* London: Constable, 1971. Also published by Sage Publications, Beverly Hills, Calif., in 1971.

VIDEOTEX '81: International conference and exhibition. Middlesex, United Kingdom: Online Conferences, 1981.

Webb, Eugene, Campbell, Donald, Schwartz, Richard, & Sechrest, Lee. *Unobtrusive Measures: Nonreactive research in the social sciences.* Chicago: Rand McNally, 1966.

Winsbury, Rex. *The electronic bookstall: Push-button publishing on videotex.* London: International Institute of Communications, 1979.

Articles and Periodicals

A British TV First! Teletext. London: Department of Industry, undated.

Ahlhauser, John W. The Electronic Newspaper: U.S. editors' reactions to teletext. *Center for New Communications Research Report, No.9* Bloomington, Ind.: School of Journalism, Indiana University, 1979.

Alexander, George. Viewdata and teletext: New electronic home information delivery systems. *The Seybold Report, No. 10,* Nov. 24, 1980.

Blumler, Jay. G. Information Overload: Is there a problem? (In Eberhard Witte, ed.), *Human Aspects of Telecommunication.* New York: Springer-Verlag, 1980.

Bygrave, Mike. Writing on an empty screen. *InterMedia, 7,* May 1979, 26–28.

Carey, James W., & Quirk, John J. The history of the future. George Gerbner, Larry P. Gross and William H. Melody, eds., *Communications Technology and Social Policy.* New York and London: John Wiley and Sons, 1973.

Chapman, Ray. The state of fleet street. *The Quill: Magazine for journalists, 69,* May 1981.

Childs, G. H. L. The situation on Videotex standards in Europe. *VIDEOTEX '81.*

Ciciora, Walter. Teletext systems: Considering the prospective user. *Society of Television and Motion Picture Engineers (SMPTE) Journal, 89,* November 1980, 846–49.

Elliott, Philip. Will there be news in 1991? Paper presented at a seminar on Manipulation in Mass Communication sponsored by the Foundation for Mass Communication Research, Koningshof Veldhoven, The Netherlands, March 25–27, 1981. Also published as "The Mass Media and the Manipulation of Culture." *Massacommunicatie, 9,* June 1981, 114–124.

Ethridge, Mark. Report from Coral Gables: We can relax. Or can we?" *Electronic Publishing: The Newspaper of the Future.* A report by the Associated Press Managing Editors Media Competition Committee, November 1980.

Eymery, Gérard. Teletext in France: Antiope-Services. *European Broadcasting Union Review, 32,* March 1981.

Fielding, Cecelia, & Porter, William C. Time to turn on the newspaper. *The Quill: Magazine for Journalists, 69,* April 1981.

Greenspun, H.M. Guarding our most precious freedom. (*American Newspaper Publishers Association*), *Research Institute Bulletin, No. 1324,* August 13, 1979.

Griffin-Beale, Chris. UK pulls together to push teletext in U.S. *Broadcast, 2,* March 1981.

Kelly, Bill. All the news that's fit to compute. *Washington Journalism Review,* April 1980.

Kennedy, George P. British videotex experience gives hint of future. *presstime* (journal of the American Newspaper Publishers Association), September 1981.

Kimmel, Hans. Germany: A battle between broadcasters and the press. *InterMedia, 7,* May 1979, 39-40.

Laakaniemi, Ray. The computer connection: America's first computer-delivered newspaper. *Newspaper Research Journal, 2,* July 1981, 61-68.

Large, Peter. European standard on viewdata is emerging. *The Guardian,* March 17, 1981.

Leavitt, Don. Study pinpoints six issues raised by viewdata. *Computer-World,* Feb. 19, 1979.

Machalaba, Daniel. Hot off the screen: More publishers beam electronic newspapers to home video sets. *The Wall Street Journal,* Jan. 2, 1981, 7.

McCombs, Maxwell, & Eyal, Chaim. Spending on mass media. *Journal of Communication, 30,* Winter 1980, 153-58.

McIntyre, Colin. CEEFAX—An editorial update. *European Broadcasting Union Review, 32,* March 1981.

McIntyre, Colin. Making news more than just a picture for the deaf. *Viewdata Magazine, 4,* July 1979.

Meyer, Philip. What videotex can learn from newspapers. *Nieman Reports,* Winter 1981.

Morse, R.C. Videotex in America: The Birth of Electronic Newspapering, *Editor & Publisher,* June 26, 1982.

ORACLE: Broadcasting the written word. Basingstoke, England: Kempsters, undated.

Pelton, Joseph N. The future of telecommunications: A Delphi survey. *Journal of Communication, 31,* Winter 1981.

Prestel User, The, 4, January 1981, 1-116.

Redfearn Judy. Viewdata systems: Battle joined. *Nature, 291,* May 21, 1981, 182.

Robinson, John P. Toward a post-industrious society. *Public Opinion,* August/September 1979.

Schultz, Brad. Manitoba town to test viewdata-type service. *Computer-World,* August 6, 1979.

Scots consult their own oracle. *Broadcast,* July 20, 1981.

Shaw, Donald L. News bias and the telegraph: A study of historical change. *Journalism Quarterly, 44,* Spring 1967, 3-12, 31.

Shaw, Donald L. Technology: Freedom for what? (In Ronald T. Farrar and John D. Stevens, eds.), *Mass Media and the National Experience.* New York: Harper and Row, 1971.

Stewart, T. PRESTEL—How usable is it? (In Eberhard Witte, ed.), *Human Aspects of Telecommunication.* New York: Springer-Verlag, 1980.

Stothard, Peter. Why instant information is slow to catch on. *The Sunday Times,* Jan. 25, 1981, 61.

Teletext and Videotext. *Broadcasting,* June 28, 1982.

Teletext and Viewdata for the World. Basingstoke, England: Bell Carter Elliot Richards Limited, 1979.

Teletext: TV gets married to the printed world. *Broadcasting,* Aug. 20, 1979, 30-36.

TV systems enabling viewers to call up printed data catch the eye of media firms. *The Wall Street Journal,* July 24, 1979, 40.

TV turns to print. *Newsweek,* July 30, 1979, 73-75.

Thomas, Hillary. VIDEOTEX: Review of the year. *InterMedia, 7,* November 1979, 27-29.

Tyler, Michael. Videotex, prestel, and teletext: The economics and politics of some electronic publishing media. *Telecommunications Policy,* March 1979.

VideoPrint, May 22, 1981.

Videotex: Words on the TV screen. *InterMedia, 7,* May 1979, 6-53.

Viewtron test shows wide usage of AP news. *AP Log,* Nov. 9, 1981.

Weaver, David H., & Buddenbaum, Judith M. Newspapers and television: A review of research on uses and effects. (American Newspaper Publishers Association), *News Research Report, No. 19,* April 20, 1979. Reprinted in G. Cleveland Wilhoit and Harold de Bock, eds., *Mass Communication Review Yearbook, Vol. 1.* Beverly Hills and London: Sage Publications 1980.

Weaver, David H., & McCombs, Maxwell. Journalism and social science: A new relationship? *Public Opinion Quarterly, 44,* Winter 1981, 477–94.

Weaver, David H. Recent trends in newspaper readership research, *Center for New Communications Research Report, No. 5,* Bloomington, Ind.: School of Journalism, Indiana University, 1978.

Which? January 1981.

Unpublished Reports

Becker, Lee B., & Rafaeli, Sheizaf. *Cable's impact on media use: A preliminary report from Columbus.* Paper presented to the Theory and Methodology Division, Association for Education in Journalism, East Lansing, Mich., August 1981.

Davis, Robert. *Response to innovation: A study of popular argument about new mass media.* Unpublished dissertation, University Microfilms, Inc., Ann Arbor, Mich., 1976.

Electronic publishing: The newspaper of the future? Report by the Associated Press Managing Editors Media Competition Committee, November 1980.

Fuller, Keith. "Report of AP's participation in Knight-Ridder viewtron project," Associated Press, Fall 1981.

Gray, Peggy. *A study of communication behavior.* Leicester: Center for Mass Communication Research, University of Leicester, 1981.

McIntyre, Colin. *BBC Ceefax girl the fastest in Moscow.* Ceefax paper, September 1980.

McIntyre, Colin. *Ceefax and the hard of hearing.* Ceefax briefing, undated.

McIntyre, Colin. *The Palantype experiment.* Ceefax paper, BB/1, February 1981, 1–6.

Netherlands Broadcasting Foundation Teletext Survey. Hilversum: NOS, 1981.

Philips Teletext Users' Survey. London: Philips Video Division, 1981.

Rimmer, Tony. *VIEWDATA—Interactive television, with particular emphasis on the British Post Office's PRESTEL.* Paper presented to the 1979 annual meeting of the Association for Education in Journalism, Houston, Texas.

Teletext & Viewdata: The commitment conference. London: Department of Industry and National Economic Development Office, 1981.

Zaradich, Linda. *Electronic home news delivery: A systems analysis.* Written for a seminar on mass media and society at the School of Journalism, Indiana University, in April 1981.

Zaradich, Linda. *Electronic news delivery: A survey of 35 projects.* School of Journalism and Center for New Communications, Indiana University, Bloomington, October 1981.

APPENDIX 1

(British Teletext Contents)[a]
Ceefax (BBC 1)

News

Headlines
News in detail
News diary
People in the News
Charivari—a lighter look at the news
News Index
Newsreel

Finance

Headlines/Index
News and Reports
Market Reports
F.T. Index
Stocks and Shares
Money Markets
Exchange Rates
Commodities
Diary

Newsflash

Turn to this page to watch television programmes—when something important happens a NEWSFLASH will appear on the picture.

Alarm Clock Page

This page can change every minute. It can also be used as a silent alarm clock. Turn to page 160 for instructions.

Food Guide

Headlines/Index
Shopping Basket
Meat Prices
Fish and Egg Prices
Vegetable Prices
Fruit Prices
Recipe
Farm News

Entertainment

Today's TV:
BBC 1
BBC 2
ITV
Radio Highlights
Films on TV
Top Forty plus Top Ten LPs
TV Choice
Tomorrow's TV
Points of View

Full Index

A–F
G–O
P–Z

Deaf News

A mini-magazine of topics of interest to the hard of hearing.

---

[a]From *The Prestel User,* Vol. 4, No. 1, January 1981, pp. 112 and 113.

Weather and Travel

Headlines/Index
Weather Maps
Weather Forecast
Temperatures
Travel News
Exchange rates

Sub-titles

A number of BBC programmes are being sub-titled to help those with hearing difficulties.

Other Pages

News about CEEFAX
Transmitter News
Engineering Test Pages

Sport

Headlines
Sports News

On Saturdays, Sport Plus takes over some of the Finance pages to provide full coverage of the sporting scene.

Ceefax (BBC 2)

Sport

These pages cover tables and statistics as well as a look ahead to forthcoming events.

Index
Pages

Features

This is the place to look for new, interesting or unusual subjects. Hobbies, pastimes, places to go and things to see can be found here.

Index
Pages

Fun 'n' Games

Every week a new selection of puzzles, jokes and quizzes to amuse the whole family.

Index
Pages

Consumer

News, views and advice on a range of topics in and around the home and garden.

Index
Pages

Finance

Pages of valuable advice for the saver— from tax tips to investment information.

Index
Pages

Spectrum

A countrywide look at exhibitions, galleries and film news, together with a What's On Guide.

Index
Pages

Reviews

This section covers a wide area—music, from punk to classical, as well as theatre, books and films.

Index
Pages

Contact

A look at some of the organisations offering help to the public including addresses and telephone numbers.

Index
Pages

Other Pages

Newsflash
Alarm Clock
Subtitle
Christian Comment
Index
Engineering Test Pages

News Background

This is the section which looks at the main news stories, picks out the key facts, and explains them simply.

Index
Pages

TV & Radio Plus

TV and radio programmes together with news of forthcoming programmes and a look behind the scenes.

Index
Pages

Oracle (ITV)

Main Index
TV Index

Starred Viewing Tonight
New Programmes on ITV
Story so far—Drama synopses

ITV Programmes & TV
Film Reviews

Anglia
ATV
Border
Channel
Grampian
Granada
HTV
London today/tomorrow
Scottish
Southern
Tyne Tees
Ulster
Westward
Yorkshire
BBC TV Programmes
World of Sport (Thurs.-Sat.)
Schools Programmes (in term)

Weather and Travel
Index

Nationwide Weather Map
World Weather/Long Range
   Forecast/Sunshine League/Ski News
AA Road Report
Rail News
Air News
Coastal Forecast

ITV Regions Index

Leisure Magazine

Pictures
Crosswords
Books — Best Sellers
Books — Reviews
Records — Charts
Records — Reviews
Film Reviews
Motoring
Horoscope
Fresh Food Prices
Recipes
Wine & Drinks
For the Deaf
Oracle Kid's Club/Children's Index
OK Club News
OK Jokes & Puzzles
OK Grids
Forethought

London Index

Regional What's On
& Weather

ANGLIA
ATV
BORDER
CHANNEL
GRAMPIAN
GRANADA
HTV
SCOTTISH
SOUTHERN
TYNE TEES
ULSTER
WESTWARD
YORKSHIRE

Sub-titles for the Deaf

Alphabetical Index

ITN News Index

News Headlines
Sports Headlines
Business Headlines
Latest News
News Reports
Business Report
Stock Market
Share Prices
F.T. Index
The Pound: Exchange Rates
Tourist Rates
Market Report
Company Results
Shares on the move
Sports Reports
Racing Tips/Results
News File
Wall Street Report

Advertising Index

Technical and Engineering Index

Demonstration Pages
Amateur Radio
Science News
IBA Engineering News
Eng. Test Pages

APPENDIX 2

[a]From *The Prestel User,* Vol. 4, No. 1, January 1981, pp. 76–81.

Bangladesh
Banking
Banking Industry
Barbados
Bathroom Fixtures and Accessories
Beauty Guide
Bed and Breakfast
Beds and Bedding
Belgium
Benefits
Benin
Bermuda
Bestselling Books
Bestselling Records
Betting
Bhutan
Bibliographies
Bicycles
Bicycling
Birds (Pet)
Birmingham Local Information
BL Cars
Blankets (Electric)
BMW
Boating and Yachting
Boats for Sale and Hire
Boats (Transport)
Bolivia
Book Clubs
Books Publishing Industry
Book Reviews
Books
Boots
Borrowing Money
Botswana
Boxing
Bradford Local Information
Brazil
Brewing Industry
Briefcase Phones
Bristol Local Information
Bristol Motors
British and Foreign Currency
British Leyland
Brunei
Building Companies
Building Jobs
Building Services
Bulgaria
Bulk Buying
Bullion
Burma

Burundi
Business Courses
Business Information
Business Libraries
Business News
Business Services
Business Travel
Buying a Car
Buying Guides
Buying a House

C

Calculators
Calories
Cameras
Cameroon
Camping
Camping Equipment
Canada
Cancer
Capital Expenditure Stats.
Capital Gains Tax
Capital Transfer Tax
Car Accessories
Car Buying Guide
Cardiff Local Information
Car Ferries
Car Fleet Sales
Car Leasing
Car Hire
Car Insurance
Car Racing
Cars by Make
Cars by Model
Caravans
Careers
Careers Guidance
Cartridges (Hi-Fi)
Castles
Cassettes (Audio)
Cassettes (Video)
Catering
Catering Industry
Cathedrals
Cats
Chambers of Commerce
Champions (Sporting)
Charities
Chartered Surveyors
Charter Flights
Chemical Industry
Children's Pages

Children's Stories
Chile
China
Chrysler
Churches
Cinemas
Citroen
Civil Engineering Jobs
Classified Advertisements
Cleaners (Vacuum)
Climate
Clocks
Closed User Groups
Clothing For Sale
Clothing Industry
Coach Travel
Coffee Makers
Coins
Coin Collecting
Collecting Hobbies
Colleges
Colombia
Colour Televisions
Colt Cars
Comment on News
Commercial Property
Commercial Vehicles
Commodity Prices
Communications
Companies
Company Insurance
Company Law
Company Services
Competitions
Complaints
Computers
Computer Jobs
Concerts
Concorde
Confectionery Industry
Conference Hotels
Conferences
Construction Industry
Consultancy
Consumer Advice and Rights
Consumer Durables
Consumer Prices
Continuing Education
Contraception
Contracting
Cookbook
Cookers

Copper
Corporate Information
Corporation Tax
Cosmetics Industry
Costa Rica
Cost of Living
Country Houses
Countries of the World
Coventry Local Information
Craft Equipment
Craft Shops
Credit Cards
Cricket
Cruises
Cryogenic Equipment
Cuba
Cultural Events
Currency
Current Affairs
Customer Advice
Cycling
Cycles
Cyprus
Czechoslovakia

D

Daihatsu
Daimler
Dancing
Darts
Data Communications
Datsun
Day Trips
Deafness
Decorating
Degree Courses
Demand Indicators
Denmark
Dieting
Dining Out
Directories, trade
Disability Information
Discotheques
Dishwashers
Disposable Income (Statistics)
Distribution Industry
Divorce
D.I.Y.
D.I.Y. Industry
Djibouti
Dogs
Domestic Animals

Local Authority Bonds
Local Authority Investments
Local Information
London Local Information
London Stock Market
Long Range Weather
Lorries
Lotus
Loudspeakers
Luxembourg

M

Machinery Industry
Machinery Removals
Machine Tool Industry
Machining Systems
Madagascar
Magazines
Mail Order
Mail Services
Malawi
Malaysia
Malta
Management Books
Management Consultants
Management Service Jobs
Managerial Jobs
Manchester Local Information
Mansions
Manufacturing Industry
Manufacturing Production
Maps (Tourist)
Marine Information
Marketing
Marketing and Sales Promotion
Marketing Jobs
Materials Handling Equipment
Maternity Benefits
Mauritius
Maxi
Mazda
Measures Conversion
Mechanical Engineering Industry
Media
Medical Advice
Medicine
Medieval Banquets
Members of Parliament
Menus
Mercedes
Metric Equivalents

Mexico
MG
Microphones
Microwave Ovens
Midlands Information
Mini
Mining Industry
Mobile Homes
Monaco
Money
Money Statistics
Mongolia
Morgan Cars
Morocco
Morris
Mortgages
Motels
Motor Accessories
Motorail
Motor Boats
Motor Cars
Moter Cycle Races
Motor Industry
Motoring
Motoring Advice
Motoring Holidays
Motoring Publications
Motor Insurance
Motor Racing
Movies
Moving House
Mowers
Mozambique
MPs
Museums
Music
Music Centres

N

National Accounts
Nationalised Industries
Natural Gas
Nepal
Netherlands
New Books
Newcastle Local Information
New Information on Prestel
News
News (Editorial)
News (International)
News (Local)

News (National)
Newspapers and Publishing
News Reviews
New Zealand
Nicaragua
Nigeria
Night Life
Norfolk and Norwich
    Local Information
Norway
Nottingham Local Information
Nuclear Energy/Power
Numismatics
Nursery Equipment
Nutrition

O

Occupational Guidance
Occupational Health
Occupational Safety
Occupations
Office Equipment and Services
Office Insurance
Office Removals
Offices
Oil
Oil Industry
Olympic Games (Records)
Oman
Online Information Services
Opel
Ophthalmic Information
Opinion Polls
Ovens (Microwave)
Overseas Appointments
Overseas Companies
Overseas Countries
Overseas Holidays
Overseas Jobs

P

Package Tours
Painting (Art Materials)
Painting (Decorating)
Pakistan
Panama
Paper
Paper Industry
Paper Products
Papua New Guinea
Paraguay

Parcel Services
Parks and Gardens
Parliament
Passenger Ferries
Passport Advice
Pastimes
P.A.Y.E.
Pens
Pensions Advice
Percolators
Personal Advice
Personality Tests
Personal Pages
Personnel Jobs
Peru
Pets
Peugeot
Pharmaceutical Industry
Philately
Philippines
Photography
Pictures
Places to Visit
Plane Travel
Plant Hire Industry
Plants
Plastic Products
Plastics Industry
Plays
Poland
Political News
Politics
Pollution
Polski Fiat
Population Statistics
Porsche
Portfolio Valuation
Portual
Postal Charges and Services
Post Codes
Posters
Pregnancy
Presenting Prestel
Pressure Cookers
Prestel
Prestel Availability
Prestel Equipment
Prestel Fun Page
Prestel Gazette
Prestel Guides
Prestel Order
Prestel Reviews

Prestel Services
Prestel What's New
Prestel Workers Page
Prevention of Accidents
Prevention of Illness
Prices Advice
Price Statistics
Printing Industry
Printing Services and Technology
Production Jobs
Professional Jobs
Professional Recruitment
Property for Sale
Property Industry
Public Relations
Publications
Public Transport
Publishers
Pubs
Purchasing and Supply Jobs
Puzzles

Q

Qatar
Quizzes

R

Rabbits
Racing (Horse)
Racing (Motor)
Radio Phones
Radios
Rail Travel
Rates of Interest
Recipes
Record Breakers
Record Players
Records (Musical)
Recreation
Recruitment
Reference Books
Refrigeration and Air-Conditioning
Refrigerators
Regional Statistics
Reliant
Religion
Removals
Renault
Rental and Hire
Research Jobs
Response Frames

Restaurants
Retail Food Prices
Retail Industry
Retail Price Index
Reviews and Critiques
Reviews of Prestel
River Transport
Road Haulage
Rolls-Royce
Romania
Rover
Rubber Industry
Rugby
Russia

S

Saab
Safety Advice
Safety at Work
Sailing
Sailing Craft
Sales Jobs
Saudi Arabia
Savings
Savings Bonds
Schedules, Air, Train, Boat
Science
Science and Technology Jobs
Scientific Advances
Sea Cruises
Sea Ferries
Sea Freight
Secretarial Services
Sectors
Self-Catering Holidays
Seminars
Senegal
Seychelles
Shares
Shavers
Shelving Brackets
Shipbuilding
Shipping Industry
Shipping Forecasts
Shipping Services
Shoes
Shopping
Shopping Advice
Shopping Guide
Shopping by Post
Shops

Shops for Sale/Lease
Sickness Prevention
Sickness (What to Do?)
Sierra Leone
Sightseeing
Simca
Singapore
Skateboarding
Skiing
Skoda
Skytrain
Sleepers
Slimming
Smoking Advice
Snooker and Billiards
Soccer
Social Security
Social Statistics
Social Work
Solicitors
Somalia
South Africa
Speakers (Hi-Fi)
Spain
Spectacles
Spin Dryers
Sports
Sports Centres
Sports News
Sports Results
Squash
Sri Lanka
Stamps
Stationery
Stately Homes
Statistics
Steam Railways
Stereos
St. Lucia
Stock Market Reports
Stores
Stories for Children
Storm Warnings
Styli
Subaru
Sudan
Sun Lamps
Surinam
Surveyors
Swaziland
Sweden

Swimming
Switzerland
Syria

T

Taiwan
Talbot
Talking back to Prestel
Tanzania
Tapes
Tape Recorders
Tax
Taxation
Teaching Aids and Information
Teamakers
Technology
Telecommunications
Telecommunications Consultants
Telephone Services
Television Programmes
Television Sets
Television Games
Television Showrooms
    Demonstrating Prestel
Temperature (Weather)
Tennis
Tents
Textile Industry
Thailand
Theatres
Timber Industry
Timetables (Air)
Timetables (Train)
Tin
Toasters
Tobacco Industry
Tools
Top Ten Records
Touring by Car
Tourism
Tourism Statistics
Tourtist Guides and Maps
Tourist Information
Tourist Information Centres
Tours
Toyota
Track and Field
Trade Balance
Trade Directories
Trade Fairs
Trade Figures

Trade Unions
Trains
Transport Industry
Transport Services
Travel Agents
Travel Industry
Travel Information
Travel Insurance
Travel Trade What's New
Travellers' Guide
Trees
Trinidad and Tobago
Trips
Triumph
Trucks
Tumble Dryers
Turkey (Country)
Turntables
TV Dealers' Pages
TV Programmes
TV Showrooms Demonstrating Prestel
TVR Cars
Typewriters

U

UFOs
Uganda
Unemployment Statistics
Unit Trusts
United Arab Emirates
United States
University Courses
Unquoted Companies
Uruguay
USSR
Utilities

V

Vacancies
Vaccination
Vacuum Cleaners
Valuation (Houses)
Value Added Tax (VAT)
Vanden Plas

Vauxhall
Vegetable Growing
Vehicle Insurance
Venezuela
Videotex
Video Equipment
Vietnam
Viewdata
Viewdata Equipment
Viewdata Services
Volkswagen
Volvo

W

Wage Rate Statistics
Warehouses
Washing Machines
Watches
Weather
Weight Check
Welding
What's New on Prestel
What's New: Travel Trade
What's On (Entertainment)
What's On (Sport)
Wine
Winebars
Women's Pages
Work Safety
World Champions

Y

Yachting
Yemen, North
Yemen, South
Yoga
Your Own Index
Yugoslavia

Z

Zaire
Zimbabwe
Zinc

APPENDIX 3

Questionnaire Number

1. Name_____2. Year of Birth_____
3. Place of Birth_____
4. Place of Employment (name and location)_____
5. Number of Years Worked for This Organization_____
6. Previous job(s)_____

7. Have you held other jobs in the news business_____

8. What do you do exactly?_____

9. What is the first thing you do when you get to work?_____

10. In an average day, how many hours do you work   a. in the office_____, b. outside office, reporting_____, c. answering letters_____, d. in "bull sessions"_____, e. on the telephone_____, f. on the typewriter or computer terminal_____?
11. Whom do you report to (if anyone)?_____
12. How often?_____
13. Are there some stories that you think you should be covering, but for some reason you are not? _____
14. Can you name such a story?_____
15. About what proportion of the stories on the electronic delivery system are from a wire service_____? From television journalists_____? From newspaper journalists_____? From press releases_____? From your telephone reporting_____? From your personal interviews_____? From library documents_____? From other sources_____(please specify)

16. How often do your stories involve news gathering from more than one source?_____
   Most of the time _____Sometimes _____Rarely _____Never
17. Have you ever had formal training in journalism?_____Yes, _____No
18. (IF "YES") When?_____Where?_____
   Degree(s)?_____

19. How important to your kind of journalism are the following skills:
    (5 = very important; 4 = somewhat important; 3 = not particularly important;
    2 = rather unimportant; 1 = very unimportant)
    a. The ability to give people a sense of the personalities and atmosphere involved in an event _____.
    b. The ability to give a straightforward account of the facts of an incident_____.
    c. The ability to show people what conclusion they should draw from a story_____.
    d. The ability to recognize "the story" in any assignment and write up events accordingly _____ .
    e. The ability to write quickly and spell correctly_____.
    f. The ability to condense long stories quickly through editing_____.
    g. The ability to write headlines quickly which are within count and accurate in meaning _____ .
    h. The ability to gather information from different sources quickly_____.
20. How important do you think it is for your news organization to do the following?
    (3 = extremely important; 2 = quite important; 1 = somewhat important;
    0 = not really important at all)
    a. Investigate claims and statements made by the government_____.
    b. Provide analysis and interpretation of complex problems_____.
    c. Get information to the public as quickly as possible_____.
    d. Discuss national policy while it is still being developed_____.
    e. Stay away from stories where factual content cannot be verified_____.
    f. Concentrate on news which is of interest to the widest possible public_____.
    g. Develop intellectual and cultural interests of the public_____.
    h. Provide entertainment and relaxation_____.
    i. Take up grievances_____.
    j. Advise and help people_____.
    k. Be a spokesman for the underdog_____.
    l. Be a proponent of new ideas_____.
    m. Be an advocate of a political position_____.
    n. Be a mirror of life_____.
21. How important do you think the following aspects of your job are?
    (2 = very important; 1 = fairly important; and 0 = not too important)
    a. Public service—the chance to help people_____.
    b. Autonomy_____.
    c. Freedom from supervision_____.
    d. Job security_____.
    e. Pay_____.
    f. Fringe benefits_____.
    g. The chance to get ahead_____.
    h. The editorial policies of the news organization_____.
22. Have the ways in which news is gathered and written changed significantly in your time?_____   How?_____
    _____
    _____

23. Do you feel there are too many, too few, or about the right number of crusaders and social reformers in the news media today?
    _____Too many _____Too few _____About the right number
24. On the whole, how satisfied would you say you are with your job?
    _____Very satisfied _____Fairly satisfied _____Somewhat dissatisfied
    _____Very dissatisfied

25. Do you hope to be working for the same organization five years from now, or would you prefer to be working somewhere else by then?

_____Same organization _____Somewhere else _____Retired

26. (IF "SOMEWHERE ELSE") Do you intend to stay in the news media or work outside the news media?

_____Stay in news media _____Work outside news media

27. On the whole, how good a job of informing the public do you think the news media are doing today?

_____Outstanding _____Very good _____Good _____Fair _____Poor

28. How good a job of informing the public do you think your own news organization is doing?

_____Outstanding _____Very good _____Good _____Fair _____Poor

29. Now some questions about journalists and their readers/viewers/listeners. Would you agree or disagree that:

	Agree	Disagree	No Opinion	Can't Answer
a. Journalists generally know what their readers/viewers/listeners want	2	1	8	9
b. Journalists often have completely wrong ideas what the public wants	2	1	8	9
c. It is very important for a journalist to be in touch with public opinion	2	1	8	9
d. It is not of great importance to a journalist to know what people generally think about an issue	2	1	8	0
e. There is a great difference between the opinions of readers/viewers and of journalists	2	1	8	9
f. Journalists and the public generally have quite similar views on most issues	2	1	8	9
g. Among journalists, there are especially great differences in political attitudes	2	1	8	9
h. Most journalists think very much alike on political matters	2	1	8	9

30. Journalists have to use various methods to get information. Given an important story which of the following methods do you think might be justified on occasion and which would you not approve under any circumstances?

		May be Justified	Would not Approve	Undecided Depends
a.	Paying people involved in stories for information.	3	1	9
b.	Using confidential business or government documents without authorization.	3	1	9
c.	Claiming to be somebody else.	3	1	9
d.	Agreeing to protect confidentiality and not doing so.	3	1	9
e.	Badgering unwilling informants to get a story.	3	1	9
f.	Making use of personal documents without permission.	3	1	9
g.	Using hidden cameras to take photographs.	3	1	9
h.	Using hidden microphones to tape-record conversations.	3	1	9
i.	Running stories that quote an unnamed source rather than giving the person's name.	3	1	9

31. In your opinion, which of these groups stand to benefit from the introduction of electronic news delivery technology and which will be harmed by it?

		Bene- fit	Harmed	No Differ- ence	DK
a.	Newspaper proprietors and management	3	1	2	9
b.	Readers (the public)	3	1	2	9
c.	Editing journalists	3	1	2	9
d.	Compositors and typists	3	1	2	9
e.	Other print workers	3	1	2	9
f.	Reporting journalists	3	1	2	9
g.	Advertisers	3	1	2	9
	Others (Specify_____	3	1	2	9

32. Are you a member of any journalistic organizations?_____

33. (IF "YES") Which one(s)?_____

34. What is or was your father's main career occupation?
    Name/title of job_____
Description of job_____
_____

35. How many employees, if any, do you supervise in your job?_____
36. What is your sex? _____male _____female
37. About how many persons work in your media organization?_____
38. About how many persons live in the city where your media organization is located?_____
39. What city is that?_____

Thank you.

Name Index

Subject Index